Friday at Three

'This book tells the heart-rending and moving story of how one woman faced intolerable violence and suffering, and found that in the darkest hour, Jesus was there. A book to encourage anyone who has known the depths of suffering and who wants to forgive. This is the most amazing story I have heard in years.'

ROB FROST

'This is a book bursting with good news, forgiveness and hope, all experienced as a reality in the midst of cruel darkness. It is a story about heaven in the midst of hell. Marjorie Humphreys demonstrates her gifts as poet, preacher and prophet in a way that will challenge and grip you. This is a life story which is life changing.'

DAVID WILKINSON

Friday at Three

How one woman was raped – and forgave

Marjorie Humphreys

Marshall Pickering
An Imprint of HarperCollins*Publishers*

Marshall Pickering is an Imprint of
HarperCollins*Religious*
Part of HarperCollins*Publishers*
77–85 Fulham Palace Road, London W6 8JB

First published in Great Britain in 1998 by HarperCollins*Religious*
1 3 5 7 9 10 8 6 4 2

A catalogue record for this book is available
from the British Library.

ISBN 0 551 03129 8

Printed and bound in Great Britain by
Caledonian International Book Manufacturing Ltd, Glasgow

I dedicate this book to my mother,
who left me a legacy of life and love.

Contents

Foreword

It is a sad fact that those, like myself, who work with the Helicopter Emergency Medical Service encounter much tragedy and suffering. People come to harm, usually by accident but occasionally by a deliberate act. This often results in cruel and seemingly pointless suffering. Yet, I am frequently astonished by the human capacity to overcome such torment, to make sense of events, place them into some sort of order and move on. For some, a period of immobility or dependence facilitates reflection and contemplation, and a realization that, often, many of our concerns are often trivial, and that above all life and our loved ones are far more precious to us than we had formerly known.

This story, however, stands apart from all others. What is unique is that Marjorie Humphreys has not only survived extreme violence and terror, but through it has come to find an extraordinary peace and enlightenment. Marjorie writes that through her experience she has come to know 'the gifts of love, forgiveness and life'.

I approached reading her story with more than a degree of trepidation. I was afraid that to immerse myself into the depths of her horror would force a deeper realization of aspects of my work that I did not welcome. Nothing could have been further from the truth. Her courage in the face of such fear was reminiscent of the bravery of Primo Levi or the Beirut hostages who bore prolonged capture and torment. Yet there was much more: as with Sheila Cassidy's imprisonment and torture, I was humbled to read so powerful a witness to the presence of God during such an horrific ordeal, and to the certain knowledge that such suffering had purpose.

I could not help but be inspired by such a clear and joyful explanation of the nature of God's love for everyone regardless of their acts, by the deep and personal understanding of the nature of forgiveness, and by the extent of her courage and her willingness to share this with us all. Marjorie trusts God to guide the direction and use the events of her life in a profound way – her story is indeed a testament to love and forgiveness, and above all to faith.

JULIE BALDRY CURRENS
HEMS REHABILITATION CO-ORDINATOR

Introduction

I have read many books written by people who have had great and wonderful experiences, horrific experiences and just ordinary ones. All these people felt compelled to share their experiences with others, in the hope that they would encourage and bring others to a closer walk with God or to strengthen them; even, perhaps – hopefully – to change their lives. Many people write books about what they have done for God and tell of their activities as missionaries or workers for the Church. In my case, however, it is different: I am not writing about what I have done for God, but what God has done for me.

I have felt compelled to write this book because God has clearly called me to 'Go out into the world and tell of what God has done for me'. Certainly, God has done so much for me that there is no way I can keep it to myself. The Rev Donald English once said that when called to preach, a person feels they are 'bursting to preach' and cannot keep still. I have been a local preacher in the Methodist Church since 1990 and have often felt that urgency and bursting feeling to share the Good News. God has spoken to me in many ways and I have always felt that it is unfair to keep these revelations and truths to myself. In fact, the more I have shared my experiences the more I have been given by God.

This book is about sharing: sharing my faith and experience, and sharing the discoveries that have been revealed to me, flowering out of an horrific incident. It is also about hope and renewal: that in a dark world where the reality is that evil exists, we *can* have hope. I was out walking one day on my own when I became the victim of a vicious rape and attempted murder. Although I was stabbed in the mouth and body, I lived through it because of a miracle. I believe I was saved by God for a reason: to share my experience of His wonderful power and miracles. Whilst recovering in hospital I remember thinking that the only reason I wanted to live was to testify to God's mighty and wonderful acts. This, in fact, is what preaching is all about, and this is what I am called to do. By preaching, I do not only mean the image that most people have in mind when that word is used; that is, standing up in a pulpit in a church service. Preaching is sharing the Good News of Jesus Christ and that can be done in many ways – through talking to friends and neighbours, giving testimony, writing about our own experiences and living a life that is in Christ.

It has been said that when a baby throws its rattle out of the pram, all creation rocks. When that brutal attack was made on me, the ground shook, the rocks cried out in sympathy and all creation sobbed. The waves of activity, like the effect of a nuclear explosion, were far flung, and the distress caused to people hundreds of miles away gave me a picture of a great stone being thrown into a lake, with the waves and ripples going endlessly on and on. Even as I write these words, ripples are still affecting people's lives.

That nuclear explosion destroyed all my past life, and I had to let it go. All that was unreal and imposed upon me died at that moment. My life was suddenly broken into pieces and needed to be put back together. But I was saved, born again into a new world, seeing the world with different eyes and realizing new opportunities. I came to see that through my encounter with death, I passed into life at a different level. I realized that with an open mind God would now make all things new, create a new person free from all influences of the past life and build a fresh and wonderful child, living only for His glory. My life is taking a radical new direction. Now I am able to reinvent my life and reinterpret the world from a new perspective. I must now be prepared to allow the core of my being to be transcended into something different, leaving behind all my gifts, talents and abilities of the past, and offer myself to God openly, to be filled with *new* and wonderful gifts, talents and abilities.

When the wind is blowing wildly, the trees rock and sway, fences batter against their posts and litter gets strewn across roads flying up on to the roofs of houses. Sometimes the events of life feel just like such a tornado and our emotions are strewn and scattered all over the place, our very being swayed and battered.

It is at times like this that we can come to a new understanding of ourselves: all the litter of our lives, all those archaic things that are unimportant and unwanted can be swept away. Perhaps metaphorically we have put those things into a rubbish bin; and with this great tornado they disappear for ever, flying off into non-existence, leaving us free and empty of the past hurts and unwanted emotions, so that God can now fill our lives with the richness of creative and extraordinary new things.

God gave me a vision of a world so wonderful and full of forgiveness, where everyone lived in peace and harmony. I believe that it was a vision of heaven. It was this vision which charged me to preach tirelessly and to encourage people everywhere when I gave my testimony about forgiveness. I was given an amazing gift, a gift of grace by God at the time of the attack to forgive my attacker. The gift was given in such abundance that I realized I was given enough not just for myself but for others too. It is important to share anything that has been given by God, and that is what I am attempting to do.

I hope that you do not expect me to say that because of my experience I know how you feel if you are the victim of similar violence, because one of the most powerful truths that I learned was that each individual's plight is unique – no one can ever possibly know how I felt that day, and I cannot ever know exactly how you have felt or are feeling. I can only tell you my story – interspersed with poetry I've written to help me express my thoughts – and hope that it will serve as a healing experience for you.

No words can describe the depth of insight I experienced that day. The most profound revelation was that I became at one with Christ; I was nailed to the cross and saw my attacker through the eyes of Jesus. I saw how much God loves that man with a deep compassion, and I know how much God loves me and how much God loves *all* people – even the vilest person. God loves *everyone* with a depth which is indescribable in human terms. There is no condemnation, even if the person does not know God. He has forgiven that person.

My thanks go to all my friends and family for all their prayers and support, without which I may not have lived.

*

Some of the names used in this book have been changed to preserve the anonymity of those involved.

Darkness and Light

Darkness emerged,
what chaos and hell
death surged
before my eyes,
revenge and hate
I now know well
with an element
of surprise.

Abandon me
in my wilderness
while I suffer
this terrible time,
making mockery
of my wonderful peace
throwing away
the sublime.

Love came down,
shone a bright light
promise of hope indeed.
Spirit of mine
soared to a great height,
liberated and
free to meet
my Maker.

Life returned
as a gift from God,
born again
into a new world.
Life recreated,
world reinterpreted,
swept up to
another planet
by God.

MARJORIE HUMPHREYS

1

Forgiveness

Come with me, readers, on a journey. Just imagine that you climb with me into a spaceship, and we travel together to another planet, millions and millions of miles away. When we arrive and descend from the ship, we see a world very similar to our own. But, hold on, there is something different. The colours are brighter, the trees are more lush and green; it's like the dramatic contrast between the dryer parts of the continent of Australia, and the lushness of green countryside in England. The contrast is so great that the flowers and trees appear in psychedelic colours. The sun is shining more brilliantly than we have ever seen. Then we notice the people. At first they look just the same as the people on earth, but soon we spot that there is a difference. Everyone is smiling, they look happy – no, more than that: they have great joy within, their faces show that they have peace in their hearts and they radiate a wonderful glow.

The difference on this planet is that everyone has learned about forgiveness. Every single person has accepted from God the forgiveness that He offers. Every single person has accepted the gift of being able to forgive others for the hurts they have experienced. There is no bitterness, hatred, hurt, resentment or revenge.

This may seem just ridiculous idealism, and it is – in *this* world. It *is* unrealistic to expect this to happen on our planet, but

I believe it is what we should aim to achieve, and I stress the word aim. If each one of us can add one little bit towards this vision, then the world will be a more peaceful and better place to live in.

This was the vision I experienced one day, when I realized that the work God has for me is that of encouraging everyone to forgive others for the hurts and pains against them. It was a vision of heaven, heaven here on earth. I believe that God was telling me in a very powerful way that I must work ceaselessly to encourage people to forgive. That is my mission, to tell of the wonderful things that God has done for me. The most precious gift God gave to me was the ability to forgive my attacker, because it enabled me to experience life in all its fullness. My job is to share that gift, to share it abundantly. God actually gave me more than enough, so that I was filled to overflowing. The overflow has to spill out to as many people as I can reach.

Jesus said: 'For if you forgive others their trespasses, your heavenly Father will also forgive you; but if you do not forgive others, neither will your Father forgive your trespasses' (Matthew 6:14–15). Forgiveness is one of the most fundamental aspects of the gospel. It is at the heart of the Christian way of life. If we are to be witnesses in the world, then our example of forgiveness to one another must be very powerful. If we are to live as free and wholesome individuals and communities, then forgiveness is essential. To forgive someone is a conscious decision, and often seems an impossible thing to achieve; it may also take a long period of time to accomplish.

I wrote the words above just one year before my attack, for an assignment to be handed in for marking in relation to my candidating for the ordained ministry. When I read those words again recently, I realized that the study I had done on the subject of forgiveness had helped me to forgive my attacker. I hold those words close to my heart.

I had always admired people who could forgive very serious crimes, and never thought I would be able to do so. Of course, I did not do it on my own. I have forgiven my attacker, but again I stress that it was a gift of forgiveness that enabled me to be released from hate and resentment, and has helped me in my journey back to wholeness and health.

Definitions of the word forgiveness are: remit; let off; give up resentment against; pardon; to deal graciously with; and to release. The evidence of having forgiven someone is that we can honestly wish them well, and that is a tough challenge. God showed me that my attacker is a man who He created and who is very precious to Him, and I was given the grace to wish the best for him in his life.

There are three fundamental principles set out in the Old Testament for forgiveness. The first one is that of atonement, whereby the people offer sacrifices and are consequently forgiven by God. The second is a word meaning to lift or to carry, meaning that a sin is lifted or carried away. The third is a word similar to our meaning of the word forgiveness today, which can be defined as ceasing to resent or to pardon.

From the very beginning of the Bible we read about the sin of humanity in the story of Adam and Eve: that sin warrants punishment by God. But God is a gracious God. God punished Adam and Eve by banishing them from the garden, but later we read that God clothed Adam (Genesis 3:21). Does this suggest some kind of protection? Surely this is God's forgiveness or grace.

Later in the same book, we read the story of Cain and Abel: that after Cain had murdered his brother, God put a curse on Cain and drove him out, but He also sent His protection on him and put a mark on him so that no one would kill him (Genesis 4:15). Surely once again this is evidence of God's forgiveness.

In Isaiah we read of God blotting out the people's transgressions: 'I, I am He, who blots out your transgressions for My own sake, and I will not remember your sins' (43:25).

In the New Testament there are two main translations of the word forgiveness: first, to deal graciously with, or to be kind and merciful; second, to send away or to loose. (Other translations include remission and to release.) Fundamental to New Testament teaching is that the forgiven sinner must forgive others. This is made clear in the Lord's prayer (Matthew 6:12). It is an indication that we have truly repented. The definition of repent is to feel sorry, to regret, to feel remorse, to change one's mind or to turn back. We are to aim towards the ultimate goal of Christ's forgiveness, and it is interesting to note that in the verses following the Lord's prayer, Jesus stresses its importance: 'For if you forgive others their trespasses, your heavenly Father will also forgive you.'

Jesus clearly teaches this again in the parable of the unmerciful servant, where the king forgives the debtor and spares him from paying a large debt, but then will not absolve the small debt of his fellow servant. The punishment is then served on the unforgiving man (Matthew 18:21–35).

It is more usual to find forgiveness linked directly with Christ's teaching than with the cross. But we must acknowledge the important fact that God sent Jesus to die on the cross, so that all our sins may be forgiven. The work of Christ was unique and never need be repeated. Christ died once and for all, for our sins. The priestly sacrifices in the temple had to be repeated daily, but Christ made the perfect sacrifice once and for all when He offered Himself. The forgiveness of sins is available to all who wish to accept and believe, but forgiveness from God comes hand in hand with repentance. In Luke's account of the crucifixion we read of Jesus on the cross saying, 'Father, forgive them;

for they know not what they are doing' (23:34). Jesus also forgave the robber who recognized his sin, and He said to him: 'Today you will be with me in Paradise' (Luke 23:43). Jesus was offering forgiveness to these people, but it was up to them to repent, turn towards Him, and accept that offer.

An important point to note is that forgiveness is the starting point of healing. In Mark's Gospel we read of the healing of the paralytic man. Jesus said to the man: 'Son, your sins are forgiven' (2:5); the teachers subsequently questioned Jesus. The message Jesus was teaching was that if we repent and believe first, then we will have faith and be healed, not necessarily of any physical afflictions, but primarily in our souls. We then will become whole and happy people living at peace with ourselves, others and God.

Forgiveness is very important for our society. The main reason we need to be forgiven and to forgive others is to set ourselves free. As long as we harbour hurt, hate, pain and resentment, we are tearing ourselves to pieces and destroying our inner selves. We need to be free to live wholesome lives in order to serve God and others.

We hurt when people ill-treat, exploit or abuse us. We trust people to treat us correctly and with respect, but, sadly, often this is not our experience. When we forgive we are providing a cure or a remedy for this. Unfair hurts such as disloyalty, betrayal and brutality can go deep enough to bring us to a crisis of forgiving.

To be at the receiving end of a broken promise can be heartbreaking, but betrayal is when we are treated like an enemy. Peter was disloyal to Jesus when he denied that he ever knew Him. Judas betrayed Jesus when he sold Him to His enemies. Brutality occurs when a stranger rapes a woman. She is violated utterly, to her very core. The most intimate act is turned into brutality. She does not know him, or anything about him, not even his name – she only experiences his violent actions. It is not just strangers who are violent and brutal, the people closest to us can be equally as cruel. We hear horrific stories of parents beating their children, for example. People can be cruellest of all to those closest to them.

After the hurt comes the hate. We hate the person for the wrong they have done to us, and it is this hatred that is so destructive. Sometimes hate divides our souls, and we experience a schism: one part of us hates and the other part loves. A wife may love her husband for his reliability and loyalty, and hate him for his destructive words of abuse. We often hate fiercely the people we love most and feel passionate about. Hate needs healing. Whether the hate is experienced in a subtle, passive way, or in a more overt and aggressive manner, hatred towards another person is like a disease, eating away and destroying our souls like a cancer. It is this destructive hatred that needs to be dealt with. It is important not to confuse hate with anger. The Bible tells us to 'be angry but do not sin' (Ephesians 4:26). Anger can be good and positive, and proves that we are alive or at least desire to be more alive. Healthy anger is the key motivating force to enable us to take action; it can drive us or energize us to change an intolerable situation, to speak out or to find a solution.

In order to experience healing, it is necessary to separate the person from the intolerable act which has been imposed upon us by them. We may find ourselves looking at the person as if they were an enemy, but if healing is to take place, we need to reassess this person. We need to look at that person as if they had never performed the act, as if history had been re-written, and so bring them back into our lives, looking at them in a new light. When we have done this we have effectively detached the person from the act. It is important, though, not to ignore the act of abuse, as if it never existed, otherwise nothing can be done to put things right.

Reconciliation can only occur when the person who hurt us genuinely seeks repentance. They may or may not know how much they have hurt us. When they say 'sorry', and mean it from their heart, and we forgive them, then reconciliation may take place. It is not always possible to return to the relationship exactly as it was – indeed, that may not be wise – but a new start can be made, as two new people are starting again. Reconciliation is the ideal, the ultimate goal to aim for. Of course, life is not always like that, and many times we need to consider whether we can forgive someone without that person saying sorry or repenting. This is possible, and essential if we are to be set free. Jesus forgave all those people responsible for hanging him on the cross. Even if the person who hurt us is a faceless being, or almost faceless, just like a stranger who commits violence, it is possible to forgive, and essential if we are to be healed. We may never see the person again, and if forgiveness relied on the other person's repentance, then it would be impossible to forgive in some circumstances. As we are reconciled to God and to one another, the love of God is then able to flow through us and out to those in need.

The story of Corrie ten Boom is a dramatic example of this:

> A Dutch woman, Corrie ten Boom, at the age of fifty was suddenly plunged into the excitement of helping Jews escape the Nazis. As a result, she and her sister Betsie were sent to Ravensbruck concentration camp, where Betsie died. After the war, Corrie worked tirelessly helping people to forgive.
>
> Then came the day when one of those sadistic guards from Ravensbruck stepped up to her with a beaming face.

He had found God's forgiveness and wanted to shake her hand. All the horrors of the camp and of her sister's suffering passed before Corrie's eyes. Her arm seemed to be stuck to her side.

Silently she prayed, 'Jesus, I cannot forgive him. Give me your forgiveness.'

'As I took his hand,' she writes, 'the most incredible thing happened. From my shoulder along my arm and through my hand a current seemed to pass from me to him, while in my heart sprang a love for this stranger that almost overwhelmed me.'[1]

Corrie's story is a moving one, yet may leave some people with a sense of indignation that justice has not been done. In fact, I believe that it is easier to forgive someone if we know that there will be justice one day, whether in this life or beyond, whether the justice is done by judges in court or ultimately by God.

Jesus evoked scandal when He dared to forgive people. As David Runcorn, in his book *Touch Wood*, says:

> He claimed unique authority to forgive sins in this world. In doing so he was claiming to be God and he was condemned for blasphemy. But he also taught that everyone should forgive – and forgive endlessly (Matt. 18:21 ff). Forgiveness, for Jesus, was not just something to do with being God. It [says] something profound about being truly human … it is tough and uncompromising. There is nothing sentimental about it. It is harder to forgive than to hate … forgiving is not being 'nice' – it is being godly.[2]

To forgive is creative, because it enables a person to move on into life again, which can only be described as healing, rather than being trapped or stuck in the hatred zone.

David Runcorn also makes the point that 'the people of the cross are those who are bound to refuse all enemies by loving them. They cannot live with the barriers of prejudice or ignorance.'[3] It is not only important in our individual lives to experience forgiveness – society needs to learn better how to forgive too. Many countries are at war, often resulting from long-term oppression of the people. Those being oppressed often seek revenge, and consequently a war develops.

In the business world, too, we need to practise forgiveness. If people recognized the value of forgiveness, then relations between employees and employers could improve greatly, and industry could be more productive. If bosses and managers would only forgive staff when they make genuine errors (obviously there need to be disciplinary procedures in place), the employees would feel free to explore more possibilities, resulting in greater creativity. Not being forgiven results in repression, and restricts one's actions.

The same policy could benefit those companies doing business deals. The cut-throat world of commerce often results in an attitude to war rather than love. Who knows what could be achieved if only companies would forgive each other and be allies, building each other up rather than destroying one another?

I have aimed to stress the importance of forgiveness as an essential part of living a healthy, wholesome and fulfilling life, and that it sets us free from the burden of emotions such as hate and resentment, which only debilitate our growth. The most crucial question we must ask ourselves is how this outrageous action is possible, especially when we are dealing with serious issues.

Surely there can be no greater testimony than that of Jesus Himself. He suffered the most horrific, barbaric punishment and death that was ever invented. He hung on that cross in excruciating pain, not only experiencing the agony of the nails through His hands and the difficulty in breathing, which caused great pain across His chest, but also experiencing the pain of rejection, disloyalty and betrayal. He was stripped, jeered at and humiliated. Yet this man Jesus was so much a human being, so much together as a person, that He could, even at that time of crisis in His life (crisis for any other human being, anyway) think of other people. This is the key to all of Christ's teaching and life. He knew the hearts and minds of others, and He knew their failings, hurts and pain.

It is only when we understand fully the needs of others, and see the reasons or possible reasons behind their actions that we can empathize with them. Jesus knew that the actions of the people who put Him on the cross were actions which stemmed from human weakness and failure. He could see through their masks, and therefore through their actions. Their lives were thus revealed to Him. We can only hope to understand partly the needs of others, but every little helps us to take one step towards being able to forgive.

We meet examples every day of our lives, some major and some trivial. The person who always pushes to the front of the queue may, as a child, have had to fight to get everything they wanted, because they may have been the smallest battling against three or four elder children who moved faster and were stronger. Another example is that of a person who never stops criticizing others. This person may have been put down by parents and criticized continually as a child. Yet we judge the actions of these people and condemn them. We *all* need healing of past hurts and pain.

Jesus did not condemn those people who wanted to kill Him, because He saw their need. If Jesus can forgive those people, surely we must try or desire to be able to forgive others for any wrong they do against us. When I was with my attacker that day

I realized I was looking at him through the eyes of Christ. I saw his need and I saw a lonely and desperate man. I saw his need to be loved. When we think about Jesus on that cross forgiving in the most powerful way, how can we not forgive people for anything that is done to us? It seems the most ridiculous thing that we allow so many trivial issues to ruin our lives. Petty arguments, for instance, about whether there should be chairs or pews in church, about which sort of hymn books we use … arguments in families over who has responsibility for aged parents … arguments over so many small things which get out of proportion. These things can ruin our lives and they need not. It is often only when a crisis happens that the trivia is forgotten, and it is often only then we realize how petty so much else in our lives is.

Vera Sinton, in her book *How Can I Forgive?*, says: 'God commands us to forgive, but He does not expect us to do it on our own. If we genuinely want to forgive the wrong done to us, He promises us His help. When we have forgiven, the wound has been cleaned and stitched, it is healing and we are free.'[4] God commands that we come to true repentance and accept His forgiveness. When we do so, our sins are lifted from us and we are set free. We can then be liberated from the burden of guilt to live our lives to the full.

I remember clearly how after my attacker had stabbed me and I fell into the arms of the man who rescued me, I was in agony and doubled up in pain. I had not seen the attacker draw his knife, but simply felt the pain in my body. At that very moment all I saw was the face of the man who rescued me: it had an astonished look upon it, as he obviously could see what my attacker was doing. His eyes were darting from me to him and I suppose he did not know what to do. This all happened in a matter of just a couple of seconds. It was then that I forgave my attacker. Whilst I was lying on the ground waiting for the air ambulance to arrive, I remember giving information to the police officer about my name and the people to contact. Then suddenly from the depths of my being I burst out with the words: 'I forgive him, he needs help more than me.'

The officer, startled, said, 'That's very brave of you. I couldn't do that.'

Yet, as I spoke those words, I was gasping for breath. I could hardly breathe due to the loss of blood and lack of oxygen, yet the words were spoken clearly and strongly and the power of God filled me to overflowing.

The impossible became possible. Looking back now I feel amazed at how I was able to forgive the attacker for what he did to me, but it came spontaneously from the heart. It is in the heart that God lives. I knew that I might die within minutes, so I felt it was something I had to do before I died. It was reported in many of the national papers, and I believe that is why God wanted me to say it, so that it bore witness to His great and mighty power. After all, that is what life is all about, and that is why God intervenes, so that He may be glorified.

The reason Jesus performed miracles was to glorify God. We read in the Gospel of John the story of Jesus raising Lazarus from the dead when He says to Martha: 'Did I not tell you that if you believed, you would see the glory of God?' (11:40). To forgive someone is to set them free, or to let them go. I wanted this man to be free, to be free in spirit. He will never be free whilst he is a prisoner of the fear of being found. He will never be free until he accepts God's forgiveness. Whilst he held me captive he thought that he was free and I was the prisoner, but in truth that was not the case. I was not really a prisoner in the same way that he was. He was frightened; frightened of being seen and a prisoner of his own uncontrollable actions.

Whilst I want him to be free spiritually, because I want him to find and experience the love of Christ, I do not condone his actions. The actions of a violent rapist, who attempted murder, cannot be tolerated, and must not go unchecked. It may appear to some people that in forgiving my attacker, I am minimizing the crime as if it did not matter. That is not so. I feel sure that the man wanted to be in control, and he would most probably have not wanted to hear me forgive him, or know that I had forgiven him. My action of forgiveness has transferred that power away from him. He cannot stop me from offering forgiveness. It was probably the last thing on earth he wanted. It is up to him, of course, to accept that offer or not. In the same way, it is always up to any person to accept the forgiveness that God offers freely to us. Forgiveness is a very powerful force.

> You have shown us that only love has the power to redeem, and that loving enemies is not passive submission to gross injustice, but is seen in the active transformation of what is wrong by a greater power.[5]

I believe that God lives in every human being. When Mary burst forth in song, 'My soul magnifies the Lord' (Luke 1:47), the power was there so strongly that all the barriers were broken down, nothing could stop it. In the same way, nothing could stop those words bursting from my soul – it was a crisis situation.

It was given as a great and wonderful gift from God, which enabled me to be set free from hate and bitterness. It was an essential part of my healing, and God knew my needs. In fact I would go so far as to say that it saved my life. Because I was positive, I kept going. The healing started right then; it was instantaneous. The forgiveness was complete, with no second thoughts and no doubts. In that one fell swoop, it was done. Likewise, the major part of my emotional healing was enacted in that instant. The promise of total healing was a real experience and assurance from God. My life was given back to me in two ways. First, in the literal sense, God saved me physically and I lived. Second, in the emotional sense, God gave me my life in all its fullness, life to be lived whole, healed and anew. Many might jump to the conclusion that I have denied the truth of the violence and deep hurt. I can only assure you that I did not push aside or bury the atrocious truth of what happened. Rather, I faced up to it, confronted it and made a decision to forgive. To forgive is, by definition, an acknowledgement that some wrong has been done; it is not toning down or ignoring the facts, and it is not tolerating a wrong action. If no wrong has been done, then there is no need to forgive. He was, and is, responsible for what he did.

Paul, in his second letter to the Corinthians says: 'But we have this treasure in clay jars, so that it may be made clear that this extraordinary power belongs to God and does not come from us' (4:7). How can I begin to explain the mystic power that filled my being, which poured out into the world from the depths of my soul? When God gives a gift it is given in abundance, and the power of forgiveness which poured into me from God just spilled out uncontrollably for others to receive.

A word of warning here. It would be wrong to forgive someone in a glib sort of way; this would be demeaning to all parties concerned and would diminish the healing properties present. To forgive is not to be taken lightly, and I must stress that it is only with that mysterious power of God that one is enabled to forgive a vicious crime that seems impossible any other way. If you really desire to be able to forgive, then God will give you that gift. When my body was broken and so weak, symbolically as the broken clay jar, the treasure was revealed. I was too weak to stop the power of God pouring out. So let it out and you will see miracles.

Father, forgive.
What, everything – everyone?
No, no way,
that's immoral – unrealistic
radical
bang 'em up I say
don't let them get away with it.
Father, forgive
the terrorists,
murderers.
Yes, yes Lord
it's tough and uncompromising
Godly.
Let them go free,
help them to come to know your love.
Father, forgive
everyone,
then I can live,
become whole,
know your healing,
liberated and free to
serve you.[6]

Notes

1. Sinton, Vera, *How Can I Forgive?*, Oxford, Lion Publishing plc., 1990, pp. 7–8.
2. Runcorn, David, *Touch Wood*, London, Darton, Longman and Todd, 1992, pp. 40–2.
3. Ibid., p. 43.

4. Sinton, Vera, *How Can I Forgive?*, p. 48.
5. Fernando, Terrence, from *Words for Today*, Sri Lanka, IBRA, 1997. (Found in *Methodist Prayer Handbook 1996/7*, published for the Council of the Methodist Church in Great Britain and the General Committee for the Methodist Church in Ireland by The Methodist Church, 25 Marylebone Road, London NW1 5JR, p. 38.)
6. Inspired by David Runcorn's *Touch Wood*, Darton, Longman and Todd, London, 1992, p. 43.

2

Walking and Dreaming

The day was beautiful. Summer colours were disappearing and the leaves were turning to different shades of green – dull and dark – and golds too; early autumn was peering just round the corner. There was blue sky, a gentle breeze and the temperature was just comfortable for walking. It was my day off and I had decided to seek some calm and tranquillity away from the bustling city life. In fact, I felt desperate to be part of the countryside once again. The concrete jungle of the city of London had surrounded me for just three weeks and my heart was already pining for green fields, trees and wild flowers. The dense population provoked in me the desire to find more spatial surroundings. Richmond had been recommended as a beauty spot, and so it was that I found myself on the banks of the River Thames, walking along the tow-path where I was surrounded by wide open spaces, vast blue skies, with the river on one side and woodland on the other.

I felt good. I had never been so physically, emotionally and spiritually fit. I felt I could cope with anything that came my way; my soul and spirit had a sense of freedom. I had felt this way for a few months now. That summer was the first time in my life that I could honestly pray that prayer of Thomas à Kempis when he talks of abandoning himself to God, opening himself to anything God may have in store: 'Lord, you know what is best. May your will decide what shall be done. Give what you will, how much you will, and when you will.'[1] The prayer scared me because I realized that God might have some very big tasks for me, but it brought also a sense of well-being and freedom, and I knew that whatever happened God would be with me. Breathing in the fresh air helped me to feel good, and I wondered how I was going to manage working and living right in the centre of London for the next two years, after enjoying living in a town in the heart of Cheshire, where riverside and forest walks were easily accessible. I wondered how I would tolerate the speed of life in London, and the density of the population which I feared would be overbearing. The way to cope, I felt, was to escape to places like this as frequently as possible. It was so important for me to feel a sense of freedom. I have always sought space in all areas of my life: physical, emotional and spiritual.

The day before had been very busy. I had spent some time with the chaplain from the Roman Catholic church, because I would be working closely with her in my new job as assistant to the Methodist chaplain for the universities of London, working from West London Mission. She was one of those beautiful people who radiates love, and I was encouraged that we would be spending some time together.

Later in the day I met a friend; I had known her for only those three short weeks but we had struck up a great friendship. She was new to the London scene too, and had arrived on the same day as I, but her role was quite different from mine. She had been sent on a placement for a short time as part of her training to be a deaconess. I valued her friendship, and had worked closely with her at a Kings Cross hostel for students over that short period of time. This day was the day for saying goodbye, as she was about to move on for further training. I reflected on my time thus far in London, feeling happy that I had begun to make some connections. I had started to build some relationships which I hoped would be fruitful in the future.

I then met up with another colleague. We chatted for a few moments, and the conversation developed into a discussion about London walks. I shared my love of walking in the countryside, and she assured me that there were plenty of pleasurable destinations to be found within easy reach of the city. My experience of walking in London so far had not been particularly successful, as the previous week I had walked round Hyde Park three times, not believing how small it was and how quickly the circumference could be covered. I still was not satisfied, I needed to find somewhere with more scope. Richmond was mentioned and that appealed to me. My colleague had been out walking that day, and promptly took out of her bag a paperback book of London walks. We found one located at Richmond, and she handed the book over to me.

So the next morning I was up early, planning my day. It was Friday 23 September, and a special day because it was my brother Peter's birthday. I am a planner by nature, and the first thing I did was to make a list of the things I intended to do that day. I thought that I must make the most of my day off, and I was excited that I could explore areas of London where I had never been before. There were some mundane tasks to do in the morning: the plumber was due to sort out my washing machine, and I still needed to think about buying some more items of furniture for the flat, such as some more comfortable chairs. Whilst waiting for the plumber, I decided to write one or two letters to my friends, whom I missed very much. I also thought about telephoning Peter, but decided to leave that until the evening. I packed my haversack with my cagoule, walking book and an underground map.

I next set about doing some housework, and took my meal for

that evening out of the freezer, so it would be ready to warm up in the microwave when I arrived back home. By noon the plumber had not arrived, so I decided to have some lunch and then went out to the shops, which were just across the road. I was living in Elephant and Castle, an area of London which is packed full of shops. My flat was in the midst of a road dense with a wide variety of supermarkets and general stores, with numerous banks and building societies sandwiched between them. I was looking forward to the day when I could explore these shops more fully, to find the treasures they held. As it was, I browsed for a while before returning home.

I decided that I couldn't wait any longer for the plumber, and decided it was time to go, so I pulled on my purple corduroy trousers, which were incredibly comfortable, a pink-and-orange tee-shirt and then my favourite red sweatshirt, which I had brought back from Australia a few months earlier. My feet were wonderfully cosy in my new little black boots, which were made of superbly soft leather, and had a good tread suitable for walking. It was nearly 1 p.m. when I left the flat to catch the number 12 bus to Westminster, where I could get a tube to Richmond.

Buses were amazingly frequent, and in no time I was at Westminster, and then on the tube heading out towards Richmond. I sat looking out of the window at the advertisements in the station; the bright colours attracted my attention. Then those walls pasted with colour turned to grey as the train surged through the underground tunnels. One station after another followed, contrasting bright colours with dark, dull, grey walls. Then there was some light. As the train moved out of the centre of London, and emerged from under ground, I could see not just blank, grey tunnels or grey and dusty buildings, but also some green fields which I had longed to set my eyes upon. Now it seemed there was hope, now there was freedom from the cramped living and working conditions of so many people and the oppressive buildings. Now I could see sky without having to look upwards, and my heart lifted. The myriads of abstract faces sitting on the train gradually dispersed, and by the time I reached my destination there were few left to stare at. I jumped off the tube at Richmond, went through the ticket barrier and out into the street. By now it was two o'clock, so my journey from the flat had taken just one hour.

I must get my map out to make sure that I head in the right direction, I thought. I began to walk through the town and up towards Richmond Hill, following the directions of the book of walks. It seemed to take a little longer than I had expected, and I wondered if I was on the right road, but eventually I found myself at the top of Richmond Hill, where I stopped to look again at my book for directions.

Wow, this is what life is all about, I thought. I was suddenly aware of such spaciousness and a vastness of sky. This is what I had been missing and longed for. What a wonderful view! What a picture to paint! There was the River Thames, winding its way through the countryside. This is what I longed to see, to take in the breathtaking beauty of nature. I noticed that there was a small park nearby, and I could see a path running along the river which disappeared out of sight. There was no doubt about it. I decided to change my plan and walk along the river instead of following the walk in the book, so I followed the path through the little park area, across a road, and then joined the path which ran alongside the river.

As I walked along I stopped to pick up a conker, and stood feeling its smoothness and thinking how it reminded me of very finely polished wood. It was so wonderfully made. Turning it over and over in the palm of my hand, I felt an immense sense of awe and wonder of God's creation, and remembered the three truths that were revealed to Julian of Norwich about a small hazelnut she found: that God made it, God loves it and God will look after it.[2] I did not fully realize the significance of those words until later; that God made *me*, God loves *me* and God will look after *me.* Oh, how important those words are and how much they mean to me now!

I put it in my pocket, intending to use it when meditating. I continued my walk, and began to think about and reflect on the events of the past years and my experiences while growing up that had somehow had a part in bringing me here…

Notes

1. à Kempis, Thomas, *The Imitation of Christ*, London, William Collins Sons & Co. Ltd., 1963, p. 134.
2. Julian of Norwich, *Enfolded in Love*, London, Darton, Longman & Todd, 1993, p. 3.

3

Memories

I ran as fast as I could, my feet pounding the pavement, not daring to tread on the cracks. I leapt up the drive round to the back of the house, and flew through the door, hungry for my lunch. I stopped in my tracks. Yes, Mum was there as always, Dad was there too, but so were a dozen other grown-up people looking rather officious. What were all these people doing in my house, sitting round the table? At six years old I expected everything to be the same every day, but today was different. My only thoughts, selfishly, were whether I would get my usual portion of rice pudding which kept me going in the afternoons. What was going on? Everyone looked so formal, dressed in heavy suits, and the table was laid with the best tablecloth and the silver cutlery, just as it was on a Sunday. But it was not Sunday. Was I expected to know the reason for this change in my usual lifestyle? Would I be expected to conform and know what to do and how to behave?

Perhaps my mother had explained to me days and weeks ago about the celebration, but maybe I had not understood or taken any notice. Anyway, I discovered that today my father was 65 (yes, I was six years old, with a father old enough to be my grandfather), and this was his retirement celebration. The members of the Co-op shop, where he had worked for many years, were all here for a ceremony and presentation. He was presented with a chiming clock for his services. I sat silently eating my lunch with all these strangers, and then had to leave to go back to school. When I got there, I told all my friends and my teacher that my father had retired today. I think they found it hard to believe me! The real advantage of my father being retired when I was so young was that I was able to spend so much time with him. I would sit for hours on his knee, listening to stories of elephants and spiders which were very real to him, as he had served in India in the First World War. Sadly he still suffered the aftereffects of malaria, which stayed with him for the rest of his life.

School was a terrifying and threatening place in my young childhood. I would tremble and shake at the sound of the headmistress, feeling totally inadequate and powerless when at the receiving end of her booming voice. My knees would knock and my heart would pound, and fear would rise up inside me, lest I could not answer her questions correctly. Any small amount of confidence that may have been lurking in my feeble little body, dressed in a navy blue gymslip, white blouse and navy tie, flew out of sight at this point, well out of my grasp. My form teacher was more compassionate and easy going, however, showing a little more love.

In those most important and vital years, I was never encouraged or directed. I had no idea of my strengths and weaknesses, or where my talents lay. I believed myself to be useless academically, with no real creativity. Yet that was not true. I did not recognize in myself my ability to read fast and well (I could read books as fast as I could eat chocolate). I did not think that being excellent at complicated jigsaws was a skill. I did not understand that my natural talent for balance – riding my bicycle with no hands, or balancing my bicycle sitting at traffic lights without putting my foot down – and roller skating with expertise could be counted, or that my skills in handicrafts such as needlecraft and cookery were important.

I was a dreamer. Often I could be found in the midst of a lesson, staring into space, unaware of the activity around me. It was as if I had the ability to stop the world and just be in my own world, all alone, where nobody could intrude. Nobody could possibly know what I was thinking – that was my own private affair, that was my escape from the world which frightened me: the world that demanded I know things which I did not know; the world which made me feel stupid; the world which did not understand me. I felt safe in my own home, but not in the outside world, and certainly not at school. Yet I knew in some odd way that I was capable of some remarkable feats. Ray, my brother, who is two years older than me, and with whom I spent most time as a child, once assured me that the human mind can do more than we ever expect or realize. I believed this to be true, yet never really believed in myself or valued myself. I dreamt that one day I would surprise everybody. I dreamt that one day I would be able to write poetry, and maybe even write a book.

Life at home, however, was good, even though we did not have much in the way of possessions. What my parents did supply to us was love in abundance. My mother was as close a description of the word love as I have ever known in a human being, expressing a love that was almost Christ-like. She was a warm and cuddly creature, always there with her apron on, working in the kitchen, baking cakes, puddings and pies. Her hair was grey, as she, like my father, was ageing – rather old, perhaps, to be a mother of such a young child. She was a martyr and a fool to herself, but she could not help but love without counting the cost. She would give away her last penny to anyone who was in need.

The Methodist church which my family attended was for me my extended family and it provided a loving environment. I never knew about any of the inevitable arguments or disagreements which occurred, but only witnessed a church family who loved each other fully. Church life brought me into contact with many people. I heard about missionaries who had gone to far-away places to spread the Word of God, and I loved to hear their stories. I vividly recall being engrossed in reading stories of missionaries who, against all the odds, survived storms of opposition and succeeded in travelling to far-off lands to spread the Word of God. I would sit gazing into space, dreaming about life in other countries, longing to taste the experience of such different cultures.

My childhood was immersed in church life; in fact, as a young child, my deepest desire was to serve God. I was surrounded constantly by the teaching of God's Word, through Scripture and also by example. Sunday School was boring at times, but on the whole I enjoyed the stories and the singing. Sunday School anniversaries are always big affairs, as there were lots of children involved. Every year presentations were made to children who moved up from the different departments, and also for attendance. At least on two occasions, I received books about missionaries, and longed in my heart to be like them. Every year, as far as I remember, I attended Scripture classes led by an old lady named Miss Tyson, and would then take an examination. This was the normal procedure for all Sunday School members who were serious about their faith.

My home was always open. Every day I arrived home to find the house filled with eager young students of drama and poetry. Mother taught elocution to what seemed like hoards of youngsters from my school, and she charged less than she could have done because she enjoyed it so much. She loved poetry, and took great delight in teaching the children how to pronounce words correctly, and how to recite poetry with feeling. Consequently she was delegated responsibility for all the church concerts and plays, and I was frequently involved. Many of her pupils were much more talented than I was, and I longed to be more confident on stage since I was shy and rather nervous. With a background like this, and with a house full of books and an endless supply of pens, pencils and paper, no wonder I am now enamoured by poetic language and fascinated by words. I am sure that I must have heard countless poems even before I was born, as my mother recited reams daily as she went about her tasks.

Long, hot, summer days were spent lazily in the garden reading books, under the shade of a large white sheet over a wooden clotheshorse made into a tent. Ray and I would visit the fairground in the local park together. One of our favourite rides was the ghost train. We would come home and re-enact the excitement, making our own fun, using anything we could lay our hands on. One day, when we were playing ghost trains, I was sitting on the front gate pretending to be a ghost. Ray was the train that came hurtling through, pushing the gate open as he chugged along. Down I fell – crash! My frail little body was cracked. I was such a tiny thing, so slightly built. I was taken to hospital and x-rayed and they found a fracture just above my left elbow. I had to stay in hospital for the night, the first time I had spent a night away from home without my mother. The next morning I went home with a great plaster round my body holding my arm in place. A few weeks later, Ray fell over and broke his wrist! With my left arm and his right arm out of action, we stood at the wash-basin each night before going to bed and helped each other wash our faces, as if we were one pair of hands, me using my right hand and Ray using his left! Winters were spent indoors, doing jigsaws over and over again, until I knew them so well I could do them in record time.

Once a month I would visit my aunties and uncle on the other side of Liverpool (the city where I was born), either on my bicycle when I was old enough, or on the bus with Ray. We would be fed like hungry lions with chocolate cake, cocoa to drink and given more pocket money than my parents could ever afford. It made us feel very rich: I used to save mine to buy stamps for my collection, or wool or material to make dolls' clothes.

My childhood days were happy and I was given ample opportunities to develop my love of freedom. Whilst my mother obviously worried about me when I went off on my own, she never stopped me. I consequently learned a lot by making mistakes and having to scrape through on my own. I was fortunate, too, that I spent long hours with my brother Ray exploring places of interest, usually on our bikes. Many times during the school holidays Ray took me out for the day, and we travelled on the buses, trams and trains to Kirkby or the Pier Head, and then sometimes on to the ferry to take us across to New Brighton, or by train to Hoylake or West Kirby. I loved exploring new places.

Peter, my other brother, was twelve years older than me and he loved me passionately. By the time I was seven years old, he was out in the workplace, earning his own keep, and so was able to buy very special presents at Christmas and birthdays. He was generous in his loving affection towards me. He would delight in escaping from the city, and cycle into the countryside whenever he could, often into Cheshire, or North Wales. I longed to be able to cycle such long distances on my own, and planned to do so one day.

I believe my mother showed a love which gave me permission to be myself. Whilst she did not encourage me in the field of academic education (never having been out to work, since from an early age she cared for her sick mother and younger siblings, she didn't see the necessity of any high degree of education), I believe that living and learning to survive is an education in itself. I do not ever remember my mother saying a discouraging word to me. She always said that we should look for the good in people, and she certainly showed that to me. I remember that she often told me that I was as good as gold, and I felt very precious to her. Now I understand why I feel comforted when I think of God as mother, because in Isaiah 43:4 we read those wonderful words of God: 'You are precious in my sight … and I love you.' My mother, though, experienced fear in a very real way. I did not realize it at the time, but she was constantly frightened of upsetting others, and consequently lived to please others. I learned that pattern of behaviour by following in my mother's footsteps, and found myself always on the alert, reading the faces of others, trying to ensure that I would never upset them. I learned never to risk anyone's anger, as the danger was too great. To fight was too dangerous, so flight was my way of coping. This fear of confrontation, born within me at an early age, proved to be a significant part of my character, and sadly, I carried it with me until I was nearly 50 years old. This fear, for I could not risk the consequences, shaped my life and relationships at home, within my marriage and in the workplace. Being driven by fear always to satisfy the needs of others is not a happy or healthy existence.

4

Growing

Bang! Bang! Bang! the door. Who could it be? I opened it. 'I've come,' declared my Great-aunty Bee. She certainly had. There, on the doorstep, with two bulging suitcases, one either side of her fat body, she stood as if nothing could budge her or persuade her to go away. She was dressed in layers of absurdly coloured and patterned materials, inappropriate for a summer's day. Her old black leather shoes were laced from the toe to the ankle with odd bits of ribbon. No stockings could be seen, as her dress of purple silk covered her short legs. The woollen blue coat with a patch of orange on one side, made to look like a pocket, was far too thick, making her look even fatter. Her black velvet hat, with a bright fuchsia feather, covering an untidy mop of grey hair, suited her formidable character, and framed a chubby, determined face. I dreaded to think of what lay beneath the surface of her outer layers of clothing. I could not bear to imagine the colours and style of her underwear, for fear of bursting into laughter. Eccentricity oozed from her stout being.

She stepped in forcibly, and plonked her suitcases on the floor in the hallway. Bee was my mother's aunt and, although she lived just five miles away, we only saw her spasmodically. For two or three weeks each summer, however, she turned up for a 'holiday'. Great-aunty Bee was a dominant part of our lives because of this pattern, and whilst it was exciting and fun to have her with us, it also created havoc as her entry was always uninvited and unpredictable. She would stay when *she* decided!

The house would be disrupted for the length of her stay. The first major workload for my mother was the change of sleeping arrangements. It seemed as though every bed was changed, every member of the family moved, so that this one extra person could squeeze in. Of course, guests were given the best place, and consequently everyone else was required to move. I was the youngest and the smallest, and so I always ended up sleeping on a mattress on the floor by the side of another bed. How we managed to distribute the contents of her enormous suitcases into drawers, I do not know, but the impossible became possible, and the uninvited guest created much fun and laughter, especially for Ray and me.

Great-aunty Bee used to sew and sew, until the machine was nearly worn out. The wheels of the hand-driven sewing machine whirred round and round for hours each day, as yards of material flew through her fingers. Her life revolved round dressmaking, which was her trade. The most atrocious outfits came together, as scraps and odd pieces of material were joined and formed into shapes. If only I had kept some of the items of clothing as a memento! Once there emerged a pair of knickerbockers in a multiplicity of colours and patches, with frills. I laughed and laughed at the thought of wearing them, but did not let Aunty Bee know my feelings, as she would have expected me to wear them for school. They would have been more suitable for a clown.

If she was not sewing, she was eating. Mealtimes were great fun: she would have us in stitches by making her favourite – swiss roll sandwiches (a piece of chocolate swiss roll between two pieces of bread). Sometimes in the evening, we would share a box of chocolates. As the box was handed to her she would say,

'I'll take two, to save you passing it round again.' Of course, she did the same time and again.

Aunty Bee taught me about learning to live with different people. She was seen by the family as being eccentric, but in fact she was simply being very real and honest about herself. She would not be pressured into conforming to the ways of others. It was a lesson about how she could be the person she wanted rather than what others tried to make her.

An important annual event for the family was the Co-op sports day. This was held at some grounds not far from where we lived, and included all kinds of races and events. My favourite was the morris dancing. I would sit in awe watching the girls, with their brightly coloured outfits and bunches of crepe paper in their hands, swaying and swinging in the sunlight. On very hot days the girls would pass out due to the heat; one by one they fell like packs of cards, and one by one they were rescued by the St John Ambulance helpers. On one of the sports days, when I was nine years old, I got up early, dressed and was ready to go, eager to make the most of this day out. Mum and Dad were not ready; they always took ages to prepare for an outing and I was impatient. I did not want to miss any of the events, so I persuaded Mum that I would be safe enough going on my own, as I knew the way and where the event was located, only about a mile away. I ran (I always ran, like children do) across the dual carriageway (our house was situated on a major trunk road), past the local shops and along a country lane. Even in the city, there were farms to be found and here, as I ran past the solitary farm, smells wafted past my nostrils from the cowsheds.

I found the entrance to the sports ground and quickly searched out the morris dancers. I aimed straight for the colourful display, sat down on a wooden bench and watched. It had started, and there they were, stepping and marching in time, swinging and dancing, all so perfectly practised. I sat, and time slipped by. Next to me sat a man, who seemed old to me, but would have only been about 40 years old. He had a bag of sweets in his hand. He offered one to me, but I refused, not being a sweet eater. I continued to watch; he stayed too. Then he offered me the bag of sweets again and once more I refused. Then came a sense of danger in my mind and he asked me if I would go with him to the back of the tent just behind us, which was selling teas and coffees. Even in my innocence, it dawned on me that danger lurked in the dark corners of his mind. I panicked, jumped up quickly and ran to the gate to wait for my mother. It seemed an age before she came and I told her about the man, but no action was taken. I have no idea what my mother thought; she may not have realized the seriousness of it because she was very naïve, or she may not have wanted to make an issue of the incident. This was my first taste of the big wide world being a place where I could not trust everyone. I was learning the hard lesson that outside my family and church, the world was hard, corrupt, and I was vulnerable. I doubt whether my mother realized fully the corruption of the world, as she had always lived in the safe cocoon of her family, and had rarely ventured outside that nucleus.

At the age of 14 I made a commitment to follow the Lord Jesus Christ and became a full member of the Methodist church. At that age, I did not fully understand the meaning of the gospel, nor did I experience any outstanding revelation of Jesus Christ or have any vision, but I made a conscious decision. I had experienced on many occasions, though, some depth of the mystery of a power much greater than myself, and had been moved to tears, not knowing why, whilst singing hymns in church. I would feel a welling up of some emotion inside, and drops would form, glistening in my eyes, running down my cheeks.

I did not understand this at the time, and I did my best to hide the emotion.

School life improved as I grew more confident. I enjoyed my secondary education, and made the most of opportunities presented to me. My mother positively declared that she did not want me to pass the eleven-plus examination. I wanted to pass, though, and was bitterly disappointed when I didn't. I was a good all-rounder, and tasted the excitement of being in the netball and hockey teams. I enjoyed all the lessons, and was popular with the other girls. I began to believe in myself, and found that I was capable of learning new and varied subjects. We planned walks at weekends, and ventured into Wales and the Lake District. A change of headmistress in the midst of my time there was positive, and she encouraged us all to take part in activities out of school hours. The shy, fragile creature that I had been in junior school emerged into a strong and confident teenager. I was honoured and overjoyed when asked to be Head Girl in my last year, and I know that it helped build my confidence, as I was given several responsibilities. My career after school was limited to either working in a shop or factory, or taking further training in office work. I chose the latter, and went on a year's full-time secretarial course, as I saw that this was the only way to escape from a factory or shop.

As I grew up into my later teen years, as so often happens, I moved away from the doctrines that had saturated my early life. In my bid for independence, I rebelled against the Church, and turned away from God. Just as mothers so often have to suffer the loneliness of their children breaking free, I believe God is equally as hurt when we tug at the strings and turn away, seeking other pleasures. But just as mothers do, I believe that God keeps on loving. I do not believe I ever cut the cord completely, but I spent many years struggling in a tug-of-war situation, trying to find myself.

I wanted to explore life in different ways; the world outside was exciting, and a new adventure in my life had begun. I left school and started work, and began to see how other people lived. I realized that my life had been quite narrow, in the sense that everything had revolved round the Church. Now I wanted to spread my wings and search for more. I met a young man, Russ (whom I was later to marry), and started courting. My interests began to expand as I ventured out into the world.

Always, though, God was with me. At the back of my mind, I always knew that whilst I was searching for wholeness and fulfilment, He was there. Something deep down inside me was there, and no matter how much I tried, I could not bury it. There is no hiding place from God, as the Psalmist says in Psalm 139: 'Where can I go from your Spirit? Or where can I flee from Your presence?'

At the age of 20 I was married to Russ, and soon found myself immersed in family life, with two daughters, Karen and Martene. During my married life I dipped in and out of church. I longed to be more involved in church life, but Russ was not too keen about going, and with family commitments and other distractions it was difficult. Maybe that was just an excuse. From time to time I would reflect back to my childhood and long for that lifestyle again, but there was a pull towards doing other things.

During the summer of the first year in our own house, when Karen was just a few months old, I was a victim of an attempted rape. The housing estate was not yet complete, and there were always workmen passing to and fro, from the hut to the half-built houses. I provided tea on occasions to these workmen, as did many of the other housewives along the road. One day, whilst I was in the kitchen, one of the workmen came along the driveway and walked straight into my house. The door was open as it was a hot summer's day. I managed to fight him off and he fled, but I was left with a mark on my face. He had been drinking. The case went to court but was dismissed. This frightened me as I felt rather vulnerable in my own house, and it was such a threatening and disturbing experience.

Long, hot, lazy and glorious summers enabled us to experience many camping holidays as a family. One way of making the most of the summer was to go for weekends into the country or by the sea. We had the packing, unpacking and tent erecting down to a fine art. The adventure of camping enabled us, as a family, to seek new and unexplored terrains (by us, anyway). The wonder of spending hours upon hours lazing on golden sands, in small bays uninhabited by anyone but ourselves, was perfect bliss. Karen and Martene were swept away to remote and beautiful places. But they didn't appreciate it fully; they did not want to be taken away from the world in such a way. They preferred some activity and their own familiar surroundings, and once able to speak for themselves, expressed a preference to remain with friends.

At one point we all, as a family, attended a Pentecostal church for two years. It happened that my daughters, then aged 10 and 13, started to go to the youth club there, and they invited us to the Christmas carol service. After that service I expressed my desire to Russ that I would like to go to church every week, and this seemed a good place to go as the congregation were very friendly. We went on the first Sunday in the New Year and it was then that I made a new commitment. I decided I would like to make a new start. I enjoyed the freedom of worship that was offered at this church, which I had not experienced before. However, after a period of time, we got so involved that everything seemed like a lot of hard work, and a real burden to carry. Russ was not happy, so we eventually left.

I was searching for some new spiritual experience, and to some extent the Pentecostal church provided the environment for that to happen. It is only now, years later, that I realize that to search for outward experience is not what Christianity is about. Now I am able to look back and see the danger of that style of worship and praise: that it slips into superficial froth, raises people up to great heights at the time, but then makes them vulnerable to dropping back down again in everyday life. It can so easily become like a 'fix'. All the experiences, though, helped me through life at the time, and if that was what I needed, then it was right that it was given to me. My spiritual journey has been strengthened in many different ways, and by many different people, all of which were being used by God.

I was ambitious. Something within me wanted to prove to the world that I was worth something. I had struggled to gain approval, to gain respect from others, and had gone through life this far thinking that I was not very intelligent. I needed to achieve something to prove to myself that I was OK. I was determined to show myself and others that I could do something well. In fact, most of the things I did in my life I did well, because I have always believed in giving my best, but something new was driving me. I was searching: searching for fulfilment and satisfaction. I tried many different jobs, but still had that nagging, yearning feeling in the depths of my being, and knew I was not in the right place.

I worked for six years in a doctor's surgery, starting as a receptionist and working my way up to become practice manager. Then I felt I wanted to move on, as this was not satisfying my needs. I looked for more interesting and exciting jobs, and found one as a personal assistant in an organization which represented private businesses, and lobbied the government on their behalf. I was offered the job, but the only drawback was that my boss declared that he was a Christian, and I felt I had had enough of that for the time being. Once again I was trying to run away from God and the Church. However, I really wanted the job, and so decided to take the post. The job did prove to be interesting and varied, and I enjoyed every minute of it. It was an excellent career move because it led to other roles within the organization, one of which required me to lobby members of Parliament.

Surprisingly, moreover, my boss did not try to persuade me to go to church. What I did see in him was the freedom to be himself, that quality of not having to live up to anything artificial. I had always misunderstood that to be a Christian I had to be better or different. I began to see that this was not the case, that I could just be myself, and know that God loved me.

I started to reflect upon the teachings of the Church and to observe the behaviour of other Christians more closely. I saw a conflict between the truth of the gospel message and the way this was interpreted by many people. It was a challenging time for me, because while I made excuses for myself to keep away from the Church because of their rules and standards, I was being faced with the reality that God would accept me with all my faults. I remembered Aunty Bee and how she had been true to herself. I wondered if God would *really* love me and accept me, no matter what I had done, or what sort of person I was.

5

God Calls

At last. My train slowly pulled into Euston station a whole hour late: the start of a typical day in the life of a lobbyist. It was 10.13 a.m. and my first appointment at the House of Commons was at 10.30 a.m., so I had to run as if my feet were treading on hot coals to the underground. I quickly bought my ticket and ran to the escalator, went down a flight of steps, along the corridor and saw a train just pulling in! Five minutes later and I needed to change again at Embankment. Another series of seemingly endless staircases were negotiated, and I made it to the District and Circle line for my final connection to Westminster. More stairs to climb, then I was through the barriers, out into the street and along the crowded pavement seething with sightseers, past the lengthy queue to the entrance of the House of Commons, through the baggage check and the body search, along the hall and into Central Lobby. Phew! It was now 10.35 a.m. I was exhausted and fully aware of sweat running from my forehead, and the fact that my hair needed brushing, but I did not have time.

As I caught my breath I heard a voice behind me: 'Marjorie Humphreys? Sorry I'm late.'

It was Elfyn Llwyd of Plaid Cymru, my first appointment of the day. I turned and smiled politely. I was so glad he was late too, and I quickly gathered my thoughts together. I appreciated the fact that we were able to find a bench to sit on as we talked.

He was keen to hear about the plight of small businesses. The half hour I spent with him was worthwhile, as he was enthusiastic about supporting one of the campaigns I presented.

My next appointment was at 11.30 a.m., and I sat waiting in the lobby for Nigel Evans, Member of Parliament for Ribble Valley. He told me he ran a shop in Swansea with his family, so he understood the problems that small businesses face. On the whole that was a good meeting, too. A short break was needed for a sandwich, and soon it was time for me to see Liz Lynne, the Liberal Member of Parliament for Rochdale. She had as busy a schedule as I did, and our meeting took place while she ate her lunch and I looked on.

After this meeting I headed back to Central Lobby, where I was to meet Emma Nicholson. The lobby was packed with hundreds of animal rights protesters and while I was waiting I happened to bump into Marjorie (Mo) Mowlam. I had not met her officially, so I introduced myself, and she agreed that we should arrange a meeting. She was being lobbied by the animal rights group and was waiting for two boy scouts. A policeman announced over the microphone system: 'Two boy scouts for Marjorie Mowlam!' Her face went bright red! Emma Nicholson arrived half an hour late, and because of the crowd in the lobby, our meeting took place in the tea room. By a quarter to five the meeting was finished, and who should I see but my boss! Whilst we were chatting Glenda Jackson walked by, and we grasped the opportunity of speaking to her.

Finally, it was the end of another day, and there were a few more Members of Parliament ticked off my list, and more support for small businesses. Most days were spent in a similar way, and the exciting life of lobbying was mine for two years. The experience was valuable and rewarding, yet at the same time it took its toll because the hectic lifestyle drained my energy.

Coming back to God happened in a very dramatic way. It was in the early days when I was still in the process of training for this exciting and varied post, and I had arranged to meet my boss in London at our office. However, a few days previously I had noticed that he had conveniently left a book called *Power for Living* on his desk, which was a Christian book. I took this book to read on the journey. It was a simply written book, and I read it all in the two-hour journey from Crewe to Euston. Nevertheless, it was quite challenging, and caused me to think about my own life. That day London was in the middle of a rail strike and the underground was disrupted. I managed to get to the office to meet my boss, but my other colleague, who was also due to arrive, telephoned to say she would not be able to attend due to the difficulties with transport. We found we had some time to spare before moving on to the next appointment, and for some reason I suggested he tell me of his conversion experience, which he did. In the space of about two minutes he explained how God had moved in his life and, in effect, very simply preached the gospel to me. I found it amazing; we must never underestimate the power of a testimony on a one-to-one basis. I remember saying, 'But I thought I knew,' and I *had* thought I knew and understood, but now I was understanding something that I had not grasped previously. I suddenly found myself in floods of tears, and all I can remember is that he prayed for me. He also said that God had some big work for me. I believed him because I felt that God was not doing this for nothing. The rest of the day was a blur and I knew that I was immersed in God's love.

God really had been good to me through my life. Since I had made a very real commitment to follow the Lord Jesus Christ at the age of 14, I had been through many trials and difficulties, but I had been strengthened and learned so much, that I felt very grateful for being a precious child of God.

We read in Scripture that time and time again the people of Israel got it wrong and turned away from God. Yet God still loved them. In the same way, no matter how much we turn our backs on God, His love will keep pouring down, beaming upon us, whether we want it or not. It is up to us to accept it, but it is there. Looking back, I believe now that God was calling me to some special work a long time ago, but I did not see it. It seems that God was nudging me all through my life, yet I did not understand, and was not open to listening to Him, or willing enough to take the risk and obey. It takes courage to act upon God's call. For years I was subconsciously hiding from the call. Eventually, though, I responded.

It was during the years of my work at the lobby group that I separated from Russ. I had changed so much and so quickly that we found it very difficult to handle. God had come into my life in such a dramatic way, and I realized that so much was wrong in my life. Suddenly, the truth was glaring at me. I was looking into a mirror and seeing a reflection that I did not like. I did not like much about myself, or about my life. I was scared, yet I could not avoid this confrontation with myself and with God. I was facing a mid-life crisis, experiencing inner turmoil and massive change. I had been avoiding facing issues in my life where I was not happy. I had been burying them, afraid to confront, afraid of the consequences. I was not familiar with confrontation, never having learned the technique of being honest and truthful in a gentle and compassionate way. There was so much in my life that I needed to sort out. I had lost myself, lost my identity, and now, like an earthquake or a flash of lightning, so much was revealed to me. I needed time to work things out, to learn to know who I was and where I was heading. It was a wrench, a fierce and cruel wrench to pull myself away from the relationship with Russ like this. It was a walk into the unknown, out into space. It was both light and dark, with fear and excitement merged into one. Our marriage did not stand the shaking and so I moved into a flat by myself.

In 1989, after only a short time of living on my own, I heard God speak to me in a very real and powerful way. I was sitting up in bed one night, not praying, not reading my Bible, but just drinking a cup of tea, when a very real power filled the room and a voice said to me, 'Go out into the world and tell people how I've changed you.'

I really couldn't cope with this and flatly refused. I sensed some kind of presence which would not go away. I felt frightened and hid under the bedclothes, but there is no point in trying to hide from God. Still the feeling would not go. Eventually I said 'Yes' and immediately it went. So I crawled back from under the covers. I had answered God's call, and was now committed to witnessing to God's mighty acts to the world. When I told my minister, he gently convinced me that preaching was what God meant, so the following year I began my studies and after three years became a local preacher.

During my studies, I experienced a time of great spiritual growth. This was the first time in my life that I had seriously studied the Bible, and what a wonderful experience it was! I found revelation after revelation, as new truths were revealed to me by the study material and by my tutor. The most significant revelation was that I realized that I did not have to take every word of the Bible literally. I realized that God speaks through the different aspects of history, story, myth and poetry, all of which we find in the Bible. That provided great freedom of thought, which was to be so important to me.

6

Moving On

I arrived back in the office, after a long and tiring week spent in London lobbying Members of Parliament. I was exhausted, because not only had I been run off my feet due to the workload, but also because of the constant travelling to and from the centre in London. The arrangement was that I stayed with my daughter, Martene, who by this time had moved to the outskirts of London; this provided very convenient living accommodation in the area.

It was a Friday morning in September 1992, and I unpacked my briefcase to sort out my papers, organized another batch of letters to be typed, and then began to prepare for a meeting in Southampton that evening. My presentation was prepared, but I just could not face the task set before me. I sat at my desk and cried. I felt totally immobilized. I could not function; I could not face this extra workload. For too long I had been juggling strenuous lobbying work and my local preaching studies, as well as coming to terms with living on my own and being responsible for myself as an individual and independent person. I had pushed myself long and hard, and finally it had caught up with me.

I went home and rested for the weekend. Monday morning came and I felt rested enough to approach the office and the tasks before me. But as I woke up on Tuesday morning, I felt

I could not face it. I felt the same surge of tears welling up inside me, and I could not contain them. They flowed incessantly and I sobbed uncontrollably. I rang my friend Joan who came to see me immediately, and she very kindly escorted me to the doctor's surgery where the sobbing continued. I was diagnosed as depressed, and referred to a psychiatrist, whereupon I was treated with counselling for about six months. Reaction to the break up of my marriage, and some other disappointments in my life were the cause of the depression, but I also believe that I was utterly exhausted, as I had driven myself hard, and worked myself into the ground for a good many months.

My time at home recovering was valuable. I began to learn to relax and to slow down. I began to take leisurely walks, along the river and in the nearby forest. Still, though, the tears would come and I had no reason to stop them. One morning, however, whilst walking along the riverbank, I suddenly, as if something surged inside me, began to stride out more forcefully, and I remember saying to myself, 'I'm going to beat this'. I walked on with a positive step towards freedom. I was not going to let this depression stop me from enjoying life. Finally the tide had turned. I was on my way back to health again. It was not easy, though, and it took a few months of determined effort, and time and space for me to relax and enjoy life.

This experience strengthened me greatly, and I learned so much about myself through counselling. As is always the case, it was a self-awareness exercise. I was also greatly encouraged and helped by reading books on meditation and psychology. At the age of 46 I was still learning who I was. Although I had felt so wretched for quite a long time, I would not have missed the experience for the world. It enabled me to grow and to search for myself, and especially what I wanted to do with my life. It also taught me the big lesson of learning to rely on God. I believe the experience to be valuable because it was the first time I had suffered in this way in my life, and I now felt able to understand better other people, who either could not cope or had experienced depression. Emerging from that time I realized more than ever that God wanted me in full-time ministry, and I presumed that was as a minister in the Methodist church.

Five o'clock in the morning and it was just light. I turned over, reluctant to jump out of bed. Just another five minutes, I thought. Slowly I eased myself out of bed and into the shower. It was another fine day, in fact, a beautiful morning. My train was leaving Crewe at 6.56 a.m. and it was almost an hour's drive to the station. Just time to eat some breakfast, pick up my case and depart. I had it down to a fine art, with everything prepared the night before, so that I did not have to think about much in the morning. I always enjoyed the journey in the car so early in the morning, driving along country lanes, particularly in the spring when the freshness is so apparent. New life was emerging in the hedgerows and the birds were singing. It was at these times that my mind was most clear, and when I could think about my life and where I was heading. On this particular morning I was aware of the power of God all around me. I realized that in my life I had experienced many situations which resulted in being able to show I had qualities to enable me to carry out the role of a minister. For many years I had worked in an office environment and was trained in administration. I had always been involved with people, and in later years, management. My job as a lobbyist had trained me to speak, and relate, to all levels of people. My job in the Membership Information Service in the same organization had served to train me for helping people in need. Of course, going back to my formative years, I had had training in speech and drama, which had helped in the area of communication. In later years I realized the desire to serve others and put my talents to good use. Throughout my life I had always found that people had come to me with their problems. I seemed to attract people somehow. Maybe I had a natural ability to listen?

Now I saw that the jigsaw was beginning to fit together, and I realized that God might well have been leading me to the ordained ministry all my life. So from that day I worked towards that goal. I had a lot of work to do to get past the first post in order to candidate. For the following two years I had my head down studying. During that period, time after time the well-known passage in Isaiah 43 kept appearing before me in services, Bible studies and books: 'I have called you by name, you are mine … You are precious in my sight, and honoured, and I love you' (43:1, 4). Also the passage in Jeremiah: 'Before I formed you in the womb I knew you, and before you were born I consecrated you; I appointed you a prophet to the nations' (1:5).

Candidating for the Methodist ministry is a long and arduous procedure, and many tasks have to be accomplished. I passed examinations, which was a relief, because I did not feel very confident in that area. It all began to slip away, though, when I commenced the interview stage. This had never concerned me before, because I had always felt confident at interviews. But in April 1994 I was informed that I would not be accepted. I had to face the truth that I had been rejected. One of the most significant factors leading to my depression two years earlier was that of rejection, and I feared the worst, that I would fall into that deep black hole again, lose my self worth and have to start all over again.

I needed help and that help came from God. I went to see some friends from the church where I worshipped, and I explained my fear. They prayed for me and God answered that prayer. God was teaching me some very hard lessons. Maybe the ordained ministry was not for me or maybe it was and the committee had made a mistake. Maybe it was not the right time for me. I will never know. But in having to face that rejection I was able to overcome this monster in my life, which God took away.

7

London

I had been walking and thinking back over my life for about half an hour, when I decided to sit down for a few moments on a small wooden bench, not because I was tired but because I wanted to take in the atmosphere and enjoy the view. Looking across the River Thames, I noticed how wide it was at this point. There were boats idling lazily in the water, large ones and small ones, yellow, red, and white, all dancing in the water which reflected the bright colours. The clinking sounds of the masts, swaying in the breeze, brought back memories of childhood holidays. Tiny, distant figures moved about slowly on the boats, which gently pulled on their moorings. One man was painting, and another was sitting on deck, reading. I was conscious of the fact that there was no loud music to deafen my ears. I could not hear the pretty sounds of starlings or blackbirds singing either, but rather the droning of those enormous metal birds that constantly fly over London, taking hundreds of people north and south, east and west, like massive flying monsters in the sky. The noise was irritating, and was the only reminder I had at that moment that I was on the outskirts of the city. My mind, though, was far from the city, and I breathed in the fresh air and the atmosphere of the countryside.

As I sat reminiscing, my mind wandered back to just a few months earlier, when I had visited my brother, Len, and his family in Adelaide, Australia. It was an opportunity I might not have been able to take again. I had decided for those four special weeks to forget about my plans for the future, and just to enjoy the reunion…

I packed my bags, not for the usual weekly trip to London, but for the rather longer stay in Australia. What would I need? I presumed that I would only need shorts, tee-shirts and summer dresses. Olive, my sister-in-law, had mentioned that it could be quite cold, but I did not believe her. One large suitcase would be enough; I was used to travelling light. I felt a tremendous sense of excitement because I was going to fly half-way round the world all by myself, and I felt courageous as I planned my adventure. The airport was not too crowded and chaotic. There seemed to be rather fewer people to board the flight than I had expected. I looked out of the window and saw the massive construction of metal sitting outside, like a big elephant. However is that going to get off the ground, I wondered. I boarded, and discovered there were lots of empty seats, but I found out that we were to pick up more passengers en route in Germany. Flying across the continents of the world was a wonderful experience. I dozed off to sleep, waking up to see the contrasting and glorious colours of the sky around me, whilst flying over the great mountain ranges of India. I remember vividly seeing the sun rise, that bright red ball, making the sky glow red on one side of the aeroplane and yet seeing the moon still shining on the other side with the sky almost black. It was amazing. I looked at my watch which I had not yet adjusted, and noticed that back home the time was midnight and here it was dawn, so six hours had disappeared! This realization brought to me once again that sense of wonder and amazement about God's creation.

The reunion with Len and Olive was emotional; I had not seen them for 30 years. We needed to get to know each other again, and so spent hours and hours just talking about our lives. South Australia is the driest state in the driest continent of the world, and I found it hard to come to terms with the lack of water. I began to see more clearly the importance that water has in our lives, and the symbol of that life-giving water brought to us so vividly in John's Gospel. I found Australia to be not just physically arid, but spiritually, too. I realized that it is a nation of people who are materialistic. Jobs, money, and possessions are the key themes in their lifestyles. Something was sadly lacking, and I clearly felt this absence or void whilst there. I experienced a sense of dryness in myself, and even though I knew God was with me, I found it hard.

Once back in England, I craved the lushness of the land. On the first day back I walked along the river near my home and marvelled at the green grasses and bulrushes which were quite overgrown. After that uncanny dryness I received great spiritual wealth.

It was time for me now to think seriously about the next step in my future life. I wanted to serve God. My path to the ordained ministry was blocked. I had committed myself to leaving my secular career of running the Member Information Department, and had already trained a new person to take over my role. I considered various options, one of them being to spend a year at bible college to be trained for laywork, and a place was offered to me. I also applied directly for some lay-worker posts, one of which was assistant chaplain to the Universities of London. I accepted that post.

The two months before moving to London had been the most creative and fruitful in my life. I was enjoying the summer and had very little pressure at work as I was winding down, which resulted in a great sense of freedom of spirit. I was preaching in my local area nearly every Sunday, and felt very excited about my future. God was blessing me, and I felt so much at peace.

The last weeks in August were exciting. I had a lot of work to do, packing up all my belongings and preparing for my new post in London. A flat was provided with the job, but it was unfurnished. I decided to rent my house but then found that someone I knew wanted lodgings for a while, so I let one of the bedrooms in the house to them, leaving my own bedroom free to be available when I needed it. I thought this would also be convenient for Christmas, as I could then host my family in my own house if need be. I left my job in the middle of August, which then meant that I had over a week to take time to sort out my furniture and living arrangements.

Then came the day of the move. Boxes and boxes were packed ready, all labelled. It was going to be a long day. I was up at six, which was not unusual for me, dressed and ready for action. There were last minute things to see to, the bed to be stripped, and the linen to be packed. I sat and enjoyed some breakfast, then waited patiently for the removal van to arrive. Doubts and fears began to spring into my mind, mixed with emotions of excitement, as I was about to launch into a new era of my life. I felt quite brave, really, taking on this new venture. The van arrived on time, and the two men did not take long to pack the load, as I was leaving most of my furniture behind, so that my house would be furnished for lodgers or tenants.

I jumped into the cab with the men and we set off. It was rather sad to leave behind a place that I had grown to love so much, even though I had not really spent much time in my own house, since I was always travelling with my job. My neighbour waved goodbye as I set off for my new life.

'Where are we going?' one of the men asked.

I had hoped that they already knew. It turned out he did

know, but was fishing for more information about why I was moving.

'Elephant and Castle,' I replied.

'D'ya know what you're doin'?' he retorted, shaking his head as if disapproving.

The implication was that I would not be safe, living in an area of London where he obviously felt I would be at some sort of risk. The other man agreed. Those doubts that had been germinating in my mind began to take root. I pushed them to one side, though, and chatted about my new job. I had by now sold my car, as I considered owning a car in London a liability, and anyway my employers were paying for my travel expenses around the city. The journey was long and tedious. It took two hours to get to the outskirts of London and then about another three to travel across it. There were some diversions because one of the bridges was closed. Finally we found the location. Nowhere to park! Not surprising, really. Still, it was a cul de sac so we double parked, opened the doors of the van, and rang the front door bell. Someone from the West London Mission was there to meet us, to let us in and welcome us. Then began the task of unloading the furniture. I surveyed the flat which was quite large, containing a kitchen, lounge, bedroom and study. The rooms were spacious, so my small amount of furniture seemed rather lost. The decor was pleasant – mostly green, which was easy on the eyes and relaxing. The double glazing helped enormously to keep out the noise of the passing traffic. I had arrived!

Now, at last, this move to London was involving me in God's work on a full-time basis. I had wanted this all my life.

8

Rape

Walking along the riverbank, I felt close to God, and wondered what He had in store for me. Little did I know what was to happen next. The time was ten to three. I came to a car park, and at that point wondered whether to walk on as the path beyond seemed to become narrower and looked more secluded and dark. But I decided to walk until three o'clock before turning back, and I wanted to get away from the crowds – that was what this walk was all about!

I noticed two fishermen by the side of the river. I walked on past them, and spotted in the distance that a figure was walking towards me along the path. He was swaggering slightly, and in the dim light I made out a tall man wearing a loose coat, his hands in his pockets. We drew closer and closer, and then when we were just a few feet apart, he stopped and asked me the time. I looked down at my watch, a watch that kept accurate time and which I valued greatly. It was now five to three, and I told him.

Suddenly – ahh! My body reeled. Something was filling my mouth and touching the back of my throat; something hard and cold; then the taste of blood. What was happening! My mind flashed – then the terror – the terror of realizing I was being murdered. So this is it – why is he killing me? I was knocked off my feet. The sky loomed above me as I was pushed into the undergrowth. I saw a flash of silver – it was the steel of the dagger he was drawing out from my mouth. Not some toy, but six inches of steel, a lethal weapon, which had split my tongue. Somehow the dagger had caught my hands and they were bleeding too.

The idyllic scene was disrupted, the peace and tranquillity of the moment were stolen, my body was captured, and a cloud of evil descended upon me as I came face to face with death. I was pushed flat on my back and he began frantically to rip off my clothes and using the dagger, ripped my trousers in two. What compulsive curiosity or fascination caused him to rip my clothes in such a frenzy and with such intensity of will? The tearing, ripping sound seemed to go on for ever. With the same sinister frenzy, he stripped himself naked. We were only a few feet from the path, in the undergrowth, where he then proceeded to rape me. I dreaded the inevitable mutilation of my body. Soon I heard the crunching of footsteps and noticed that someone was walking by on the path. I saw a figure of a man but thought it unwise to shout or raise any alarm at this point. I knew only too well that I was in the hands of a killer, and the only way to survive was to comply with his wishes and demands, and hold on to the hope that somehow I would survive this torment. I had no choice but to relinquish my resistance to the obscenities of rape. He ordered me to keep quiet.

Like a wild tiger capturing its prey, he pounced upon me and played with me. Adrenalin flowing freely, his body was tense, his eyes darting and alert, continually flashing in all directions. He was tuned up and ready to make the kill should I attempt to move. And with a lethal dagger as a weapon, what else could I do but comply to his commands?

It was at this point that I felt my preparation for such an event in life was of vital importance. Psychologists have discovered that those people who cope best are the people who have thought through events that may occur and are in some way prepared, and then, in an emergency, the mind falls naturally into some sort of pattern of behaviour. I had always known that I was vulnerable, and had decided that the best way to cope in a rape situation would be to submit, and to hope that it would soon be over and the attacker would then go. However, I never for one moment imagined that I was at risk at this point in my life, that anyone would want to rape me at my age – 48 years old. I was wrong, but it was not so much about rape as it was about violence and murder. I found myself being quite composed, in an odd sort of way, and experiencing a certain level of serenity in the situation and thinking 'Oh, so this is what it feels like to be raped'! I was well aware I might not live to tell the tale, and my thoughts wandered to how other women must have felt in this situation. Yet, although I was calm, in some strange way I felt at the same time intense waves of fear beneath the surface, far, far down in the depths of the ocean of my being, fear of the unknown irrational behaviour of this beast. But even further down, like a tiny pearl, lay peace, the pearl of peace which nothing could shake or take away.

The pearl of peace lay
beneath the thick black
cloud of fear.
Such thickness and sudden
blackness emitted from
high chimneys
which poisons the air
and spoils the pale winter sky and
the landscape
white with snow.
Contrast and conflict.

The pearl of peace lay
unmoved and unshaken
rich in that oyster shell
at the bottom
of the ocean.

My attacker was suddenly disturbed – he had noticed a man walking along the path quite close to where I lay. The attacker realized we may be noticed from the pathway, so he decided to drag me away further into the woodlands. He pulled and pushed me through the undergrowth, with my trousers trailing behind me, attached only by a few threads around my ankles, until he found a place which satisfied him, where the rape continued. He was naked apart from the tattoos which decorated his body. It was at this point that I was able to see the dagger properly and notice the detail, as he had stuck it into the ground by his side. It was here that I was able to take in and try to remember an accurate description of the man. He was vacant in some sense, in that he was not completely aware of my presence, almost as if I was a nothingness. I was being treated as totally insignificant and unimportant. If ever I was to survive this ordeal, I wanted to be able to give as much information as possible to the police. I was detesting this imposed and uninvited intimacy upon me, this hideous obscenity which was intolerable.

Yet, even in the midst of this horrific scene, it was here that I noticed how beautiful the place was: the green woodland, the trees, the leaves blowing softly, the blue sky above with a few puffy clouds and the sun shining through the tree above. For a few moments it seemed as if time stopped, as I drank in the beauty of this place. I asked him if he believed in God, and he said he did but that he needed revenge. So it was revenge that drove him to do this heinous thing to me. I could not ask him more. He disallowed my questions and conversation by his stark, cold look and uneasy, disturbed expression. Then along another path which wove through the woodlands, someone else walked by. I lay still as I watched out of the corner of my eye a male figure, but I could not see the detail. I found it hard to believe that we were so close to people enjoying their afternoon walks, unaware of my predicament, but I was in no position to escape or to cry for help. I dared not ask if he was intending to kill me. This might provoke a violent response, and yet I did not expect him to tell me the truth. Something stopped me from asking the question. I found myself experiencing intrusion, someone stepping over the boundary into my world, into my private corner, but I could not stop it. I desperately wanted the rape to stop, but I was powerless.

Eventually he decided to move me again. He told me he was going to take me somewhere else to get me cleaned up, as I was covered in blood from my tongue and hands which I had wiped on my legs. I did not for one moment believe him. I felt sure now he was planning to get rid of my body after he had killed me. I had worked out the logic of the situation, and realized that he would not want me to live to be able to describe him, as he had not hidden his identity. I had also realized what a violent man he was, with no regard for human life. His cold indifference to my humanity spoke of his disturbed mentality. He dragged me back across the same route and we retraced our steps back to the path. As soon as we were back on the original path I noticed someone coming the other way. I had to make a decision quickly. Should I try to escape? The attacker's hand gripped mine tightly and he was walking fast, so fast that I was having to almost run to keep up. As we came closer to this other man he began to walk faster and faster; obviously he was disturbed and he started running. I decided to try to make a break as I was sure

I could wriggle my hand free. As we got closer to this other man I tried to release my hand and at the same time said clearly but quietly, 'Help! I've been attacked!'

My hand did not break free, it hadn't worked. The attacker gripped me tighter – he had been ready for this. I found myself looking at this other man who was barely a foot from me, and saw his eyes dart from me to my attacker and back again several times; he was frozen to the spot for just a few seconds, but it seemed like an age. I saw a look of horror on his face. Then pain surged through my body. I realized that the dagger had been plunged into my body, fully thrust into me. I didn't see it happen – I just collapsed into the arms of my rescuer as the rapist ran off like the wind.

I had, as a woman, experienced mental, emotional, psychological and educational rape but never physical rape. The broad term of rape has been used widely in recent times not just for the physical, sexual, lustful abuse of a person, but for the abuse and disrespect of people in other areas of life. When people are not given the opportunities that are due to them in life with regard to education, and when people are victims of emotional blackmail, this is rape. I had also experienced violence of mind and emotion, but never physical violence. It shocked me to the core that someone could attempt to kill just for the sake of satisfying their animal lust. But I survived, thanks to the man who came to my rescue. I survived thanks to God. I survived and can now say that it was a privilege to have experienced and survived such an horrific incident as it brought me face to face, not only with evil, but with God. I experienced horror and glory simultaneously. Just as we see Jesus on the cross, we see the horror of it all, but if we look through that awful pain and agony, we see the glory of God and the resurrection.

In his book *Water Into Wine*, Stephen Verney says:

> Jesus on the cross will become our symbol, pointing us down into those depths of horror where human beings torture one another in prison camps – into that abyss of anguish where we experience what it is to be abandoned and where we come to know that human life doesn't make sense – and pointing us deeper still, so that we see shining out of the horror the glory of love, and we receive out of that anguish the transforming power of love.[1]

I could ask the question 'why?' for the rest of my life, and find myself unproductively going round in circles, endlessly struggling to find an answer. I believe it is more important to think about how God can work within such a situation, and try to find Him in the midst of it all.

Not only did I see God in action in the man who came to rescue me, but strangely I saw something of God in the man who attacked me, in the sense that I believe God lives in and loves *every* human being. I have heard preachers say many times that if Jesus were here today He would be found not in the churches amongst the clergy and bishops, but amongst the drug addicts and prostitutes on the streets, amongst the thieves and the murderers. My encounter with this evil man brought me to the realization that I was experiencing the company of one who was rejected, abandoned, abused and hated and, of course, Jesus knew all about these.

Let me clarify what I mean when I say I saw something of God in my attacker: I realize that sometimes we are aware of God in our lives, and sometimes we are not. Whether we realize it or not God is pouring down love on us constantly. Consequently, we can be subconsciously receiving from Him, and experiencing Him through all aspects of life at all times. It is possible to see God through many channels, and through all of creation. Behind the façade of such a tough exterior lay someone who was very hurt and damaged, and that fact would be hidden from most people. I was privileged to see through this exterior as if it was transparent, and I saw sensitivity hiding beneath the surface. I also sensed a massive amount of fear within my attacker. When a person stares at the sun, and then looks around, they see the sun in everything else. In the same way, if we look to God, we will see something of God in all people and all creation.

What a rapturous chorus of emotions had enveloped me while I was being raped. Hell and chaos in action fighting to win against the heaven of creation, the green woodland singing, the blue sky and the gentle breeze dancing softly in the trees. How could this horrific and bloody battle have been happening in the midst of such wonder and beauty? The reality was that a mixture of heaven and hell was the truth of the moment. Whilst I was experiencing the ultimate act of violation against my body, I was also experiencing the glory of God through creation. The sinister, convulsive power my attacker emitted was weak in comparison with the power that God mystically moved upon the scene. I was feeling quite alone and abandoned because I knew that I was facing almost certain death which, strangely, I readily accepted. When the time comes to die, the most important thing to centre on is the fact of dying, as that is all there is to do. My experience was that of abandonment, with a little ray of hope flashing every now and again that I might escape, somehow, from the hands of my attacker.

To face death like this was an enlightening experience. The strange thing is that I was not frightened – not of death, anyway. Certainly, I was frightened of the pain that might be imposed upon me, and the unpredictability of my immediate future, but not of death. In fact, death seemed to be warm and welcoming. Perhaps that was because I longed to be with God wholly and completely. It was as if I was about to experience a completeness, a being with God.

As I had looked up into the tree gently blowing in the breeze, I experienced one of those wonderful encounters when one glimpses eternity, when one feels that mutual awareness, being merged and absorbed into creation. Just for a few moments I soaked in that awesomeness of the presence of God in creation. The sun had shone through the leaves of the tree down on to the face of my attacker. I remembered that verse in Genesis: 'The earth was a formless void and darkness covered the face of the deep, while a wind from God swept over the face of the waters' (1:2). The Spirit or the wind of God was hovering over the chaos and hell that I was experiencing. As at creation when God composed order out of disorder, I was aware of a presence hovering over the mess and disorder. I was encouraged by the fact that I seemed to be encountering the effect of the Holy Spirit in the wind and God's love in the sunlight. This moment was a great and wonderful experience, because in that shaft of light beaming down upon the face of my attacker I saw the face of the risen Christ. That divine love was obscuring his humanity. The face of Christ was overpowering the man, covering him. That light and power was from another world. This was a moment of timelessness, when I was absorbed into another world. It is very difficult to express in words this occurrence; all I know is that it was something beyond this world and beyond human expression! Somehow it was as if the veil had been taken away, revealing the next world or the other world to which we will go. Many people have experienced a oneness with God at times in their lives when time apparently stops. In psychological terms this is sometimes known as an altered state of awareness. I knew that no matter what my attacker was doing to me, he could not contaminate me. It was as if I was being cleansed as it was happening, and God was reassuring me that it was all right.

Since that time, these words have come to me to describe that moment:

I saw the face
of the Risen Christ
beaming as light
through a tree.
Divine Love.
Obscuring the face
of the evil act
being imposed
upon me.
I saw the face
of the Risen Christ
a glimpse of
Eternity.

I hung on to the thread of hope that God would not let me down. Hope is faith in what we cannot see, and yet I was seeing with my own eyes a glimpse of eternity.

I believe that God was with me in all of this. God was with me in the suffering, the humility, the captivity. Strange though it may seem, God was also with me in my feelings of aloneness and abandonment. When I was feeling abandoned I think it must have been similar to what those first disciples experienced the night when Jesus was captured. Imagine how the disciples felt after Jesus had died on the cross. I am sure they would have felt an emptiness, a void, as though they had been completely deserted. The whole city would have been affected, and there would have been disturbed feelings of insecurity and lostness. They must have been confused and frustrated as they saw hope slip away, the hope of a wonderful future. All that they had built their lives upon was suddenly gone.

Jesus would have experienced this feeling on the cross when he called out to God: 'My God, my God, why have you forsaken me?' (Mark 15:34), but our faith is not based on feelings. Our faith is based on knowing that God is with us in every situation. God is with us in our solitude because He lives within us. I knew God was with me whatever happened. It really did not matter about my body, and how that was being abused, because my body is only temporal. I do know that our bodies are the temple of the Holy Spirit and are very precious, but in that instance, what mattered was that I was at one with God.

My body may have been in hell, captured, abused and violated, but my spirit was in heaven. There was no way my attacker could capture, abuse or violate my spirit and that was my hope. Even if he had been successful in killing me, my spirit was free, soaring above on the wings of Christ Jesus, my saviour.

Notes

1. Verney, Stephen, *Water Into Wine*, London, Darton, Longman & Todd, 1995, p. 48.

9

Rescue

God was already putting into operation a rescue plan for me, although I was not aware of it at the time. That rescue happened in a remarkable way, and in fact there are three parts to the miracle which saved me. Not only did someone come to my aid, but the Helicopter Emergency Service also saved my life because of their speed and efficiency, and then I learned from the surgeon that my physical injuries were a hair's-breadth away from being fatal.

Shot through the Bible are stories of God rescuing people, liberating them out of slavery and into freedom. I remember vividly, as a child, hearing the story of Moses leading the Israelites, and the mighty miracle of the parting of the Red Sea. I did not understand then the fullness of this story, but as I have grown in faith and studied the Bible I have realized that the miracle of the Red Sea parting was just part of a much vaster rescue operation. I have also realized that although God is all powerful and can and does perform miracles, the normal course of action is that He leads through wise leadership, through people. It is often due to the wisdom of the leader that correct decisions are made on behalf of others. The Exodus is the exciting story of God's guidance and this theme is carried through the Bible and can be witnessed today.

I also remember learning about Jesus and that He died on the cross for me. I did not then understand the fullness of the gospel message, although I did always want to be a follower. Now I understand more fully the wonderful depth of the truth and how God fulfilled His plan of ensuring liberation for all people. This is a wonderful and mighty gift, that is freely on offer to all people.

How wonderful, then, that today we can witness God rescuing people and setting them free, and my experience has been that I witnessed one such event at first hand. I was in the midst of a crisis, a victim at the hands of a killer, and God rescued me, using power and wisdom through another person. When I was lying on the ground, my body being violated, I looked up into the tree and saw the sun shining through, the leaves gently blowing in the soft breeze, and suddenly knew that the Spirit of God was hovering over all this mess, the bloody mess that I was in. God surely was there, and I experienced His glory through creation. I felt very alone and abandoned as far as my body was concerned. I knew in my conscious mind and my subconscious mind that the man intended to kill me. I was aware that I might be living my last few minutes on this earth and I began to get concerned that nobody would know where I had gone, that there would be no trace of me. Even though I felt so alone, I just hung on to a little thread of hope that I may be able to escape, somehow. It was strange that I did not cry out to God for help, and I find it rather amusing when I look back that I did not even think in my mind 'What are you doing about it, God?' In a strange way I just seemed to accept the situation.

In fact, God *was* doing something during that time, but I was not aware of the plan. God was to put into action a rescue operation, and I will never cease to be amazed at it. The time was 2.55 p.m. Across the river a lived man named Cecil who was sitting on his balcony having a drink. Let me summarize how he later explained what he saw: 'Well, I was just enjoying the sunshine, relaxing with a drink on my balcony. It was one of those perfect days for working on my boat and that is what I had been doing. Next moment I heard a scream. I looked up and couldn't believe my eyes because I saw, straight across the river, a man pushing a woman into the undergrowth. Without a moment's hesitation, because I knew she was in trouble, my mind raced as to how I could help. A boat – yes, I needed a boat to get across to help. I ran down to the riverbank and there were no boats there to jump into readily, so I frantically searched, running desperately. Finally I found a dinghy, quickly jumped into it and rowed as fast as I could to the other side. I then began to search for this woman.'

It was at this point that my attacker had finished raping me and told me that he was taking me somewhere to get me cleaned up. As he dragged me back along the original path, at approximately 3.15 p.m., I met my rescuer, Cecil. This is how his story continues: 'Eventually, as I was walking along the tow-path, I saw them coming towards me; he was dragging her behind, walking at a fast pace. Then there I was face to face with them and she looked in a mess with blood on her face, hands and legs. She tried to struggle free, but I watched, horrified, as he drew his dagger and stabbed her. I just stood there and watched helplessly. Then he ran off at great speed.'

I fell into Cecil's arms, who then laid me down on the ground on my back – the haversack I still carried providing a cushion for me – and promptly yelled at the top of his voice across the river for someone to call the police and ambulance. I will never cease to be amazed that in London someone cared enough to come and help a stranger. He certainly was a very special person, a very special Good Samaritan. God made sure that the right person saw me, a person who not only took action, but put his own life at risk, a person who was sensible enough to cope and to deal with the situation appropriately. I felt safe and secure, knowing that he had control of the situation. The amazing thing also is that I could have missed meeting him by seconds. The timing was perfect. Just as God allowed free will to the man who attacked me, God also allowed free will to the man who came to my aid. He saw the need and was brave and courageous enough to act. He acted with wisdom and courage as he knew the danger he was facing. I will never underestimate the fact that he risked his life for me.

The second part of my miracle started at 3.23 p.m. that afternoon. A 999 call had just come through to the London Ambulance headquarters. The call was assessed by the operator as 'Send police and air ambulance to Ham Common. Stabbing. Serious.'

It was now 3.28 p.m. and the red phone rang in the Helicopter Emergency Medical Service operations room, amplified so that the shrill bell rang on the helipad, alerting everyone to the fact that the helicopter was about to launch. The pilot raced out and started the engine. The crew gathered, the paramedic and a doctor boarded. The second pilot collected the computer print-out, specifying details of their destination and jumped on board. The helicopter rose up into the sky, off and away to the scene arriving at 3.36. It landed on the nearest clearing where I had been dragged across only minutes earlier. The doctor and his team ran across the clearing and through the rough terrain.

The doctor then assessed my condition, gave me oxygen, fluids via an intravenous line and analgesia. A vacuum mattress – to ensure I was protected – was used to transport me in the dash across the woodland lifting me up on to the helicopter. Twenty-two minutes after landing the HEMS team were ready to leave.

On the flight across London to the Royal London Hospital, the doctor and pilot radioed ahead to inform the Helipad and the A & E department that I was on board, gave medical details to prepare the emergency trauma team and gave the estimated arrival time. We actually arrived at 4.05 p.m.

Thus ended the second part of the miracle which saved my life: the speed of the rescue. HEMS arrived at the scene very quickly. It took only seven minutes for the helicopter to take me from the scene of the crime to hospital and even then the doctor, Steve Bree, was apparently urging the pilot to travel faster. I did not hear about this until much later, and of course it would have worried me if I had heard him uttering those words. I thank God for the expertise of the helicopter crew working so speedily and efficiently. I was in their hands completely and never before had I experienced living each second so vividly. I could not think of more than that, not the future or the past. My energies were being used in surviving the moment and no more. I believe Steve Bree was a very special person. I knew I could trust him completely, as I could sense something about him which enabled me to know that I was in his hands, and I need not worry. All I could do was lie there. He kept talking to me to try to keep me conscious and reassure me, but I drifted in and out of consciousness and the whole affair is a bit blurred. However, I do remember arriving at the hospital where there was a trauma team waiting. The surgeon confirmed that if it had not been for the speed of the helicopter, I would have died.

The imagery of the helicopter rescuing me is comparative to that of God stretching a great hand down to pick me up. In no way do I imagine God to be physically 'up there', and for us human beings to be physically 'down here', as if we were constantly separated from each other. God is with us, within everything here on earth and there is nowhere we cannot find Him. God continually enters into the hell of this world, so that we may be lifted up. The action of the helicopter was powerful and vertical, it lifted me heavenwards, to safety and away from the mess and the chaos. All those hands who saved me were the hands of God. All those faces I saw were the faces of Christ. Then when I landed on the Helipad on the roof of the hospital, still the imagery continued; it was as if I was being held up and sustained.

The third part of the miracle was the fact that I did not die from the stab wound in my body. I learned from the surgeon that the dagger had just missed my aorta by 1 millimetre. Even so I was seriously injured, and came close to death. The main damage was to my liver, which is why I lost such a lot of blood. The surgeon explained that the exact circumstances were crucial with regard to my life. For example, so much depended on what was damaged in relation to whether I was breathing in or out at the time of the injury. The fact is that I was a moving target, and so anything could have happened. I do not know whether I was breathing in or out, but obviously I was doing whatever enabled the dagger to miss my aorta by a hair's-breadth. The surgeon also told me the dagger had stopped just short of my spinal cord. I could so very easily have been disabled. I believe, though, that God was making it very clear to me that I needed to be on my feet, for whatever task was to be set before me. I was also suffering from the stab wound in my mouth and my tongue was split, but that was minor compared to the other injuries.

My experience in this one particular incident of God's saving power was threefold, and He used both the wisdom of people, and His amazing intervening power. I do not remember any more until I awoke to hear a nurse saying 'It's all over.'

But it was not all over, it was the beginning of a long haul and the beginning of new life for me. I was alive.

10

Healing

I awoke. The world was hazy. My eyes opened and closed and I drifted in and out of sleep. I was very peaceful and relaxed. I wondered if I was dreaming. Detectives and police doctors were talking quietly about forensic examination. Everything went hazy, then sleep crept upon me once more. Karen and Martene, my two daughters, appeared in the haze. Nothing was said, then they were gone. The night was long and memorable. Angela, the nurse, sat holding my hand for long hours, silently caring and suffering with me and for me. She was like my guardian angel for that special time. I appreciated this great truth later; that so many people suffered for me and with me, which lifted the burden immeasurably. They carried the weight of my pain. Never before had I experienced this aspect of suffering for others, but now it was real. It powerfully dawned upon me that the world is at one, united, linked. Every person, every part of creation, is one. Ultimately, we are all responsible for one another.

When morning light dawned I had slept little, having spent the night in some sort of daze. I was surprised when the police detective arrived at my bedside that morning and I wondered why she wanted to see me. Slowly it occurred to me that the matter was serious, that it was no dream. This was real. It had not entered my head that she would need to speak to me. My whole being was concerned with only one thing: survival. All my energies, mental and physical, were turned inward to keep myself alive. There was no extra or spare energy for thoughts beyond myself. However, the detective needed my statement, and so that long haul began. Hours upon hours were spent: a total of twenty-five hours over a period of six days, talking through every aspect and every minute detail of the whole incident. Each day the detective would wheel me away to a quiet room, where she slowly and patiently wrote down all the details of the incident. She was trained to deal with traumatic cases and was very sensitive, yet was able to gather the right information. I was lucid and I was pleased with myself for recalling details I had feared I would forget; I wanted to help the police as much as possible. It was not a problem for me to talk about what had happened, but I tired easily, which was not surprising after such a traumatic event and major surgery. I was grateful when that task was complete; it was a great relief to release it from my mind. I was grateful, too, when the pressure was taken from me to present a Photofit of the man, as this had already been done by the man who came to my rescue.

Suddenly I was deluged with mail and flowers. The mail seemed to multiply each day. I remember vividly how each day the smiling nurse walked towards me with a great pile of letters and cards. I would spend at least an hour opening my post and found great comfort from reading letters and kind words from so many people. The tears flowed readily as I read words of comfort. I learned that my friends from the church I attended in my home town in Cheshire had called a special meeting and had gathered together to pray for me. Again I felt the weight being lifted from me. Flowers arrived. Splashes of yellow, orange, pink, purple and blue were dashed around the ward. Roses, carnations and freesias overtook the ward and spilled along the corridor. The beautiful colours and perfume symbolized a source of healing, hope and new life. I did not realize I had so many friends. I was grateful for all the prayers, and realized that I was floating on the wings of prayer and being carried along by the presence of God. The truth that overwhelmed me was that so many people were suffering for me, on my behalf, which relieved me from that great weight. I was forced to rely totally on others, since I was so ill and weak.

I was beginning to feel the need for some time of solitude, even though I was afraid to be in a side ward for fear my attacker would find me, so that I could reflect on the happenings and be quiet. So many people, though, wanted to come to visit me and I could not refuse, even though I didn't have much energy. I was torn between the need to isolate myself completely as part of my need to survive emotionally, and the need to be with people I could share my thoughts with. I could only cope with a limited amount of visitors, and the police occupied most of that time with their necessary questions. Reluctantly, I asked that no visitors see me apart from my daughters.

It was on the third day of my stay that Russ came to see me. It was now four years since our divorce and I had not seen him during that time. Little did I know that this would be the start of a new friendship, one born out of the horror. The old had gone and now we were two different people. The meeting was brief but significant.

My life had been saved; I was still here, living on this earth, and I was extremely grateful for that. When the press wanted a statement I declined as I did not have the energy. How I wished I had. Instead, I sent a message to ask them to report the fact that I had forgiven the man who attacked me. I just felt so grateful that I was alive, and that I was left with no apparent permanent disability. God had saved me, and as I thought about it I realized that God had most probably spared me for a reason; to testify to the miracle that He had saved me. That was enormous. I remember lying in my hospital bed and speaking these words to someone: 'The only reason I want to live is to tell of God's mighty acts.' Those words rang in my ears for months afterwards. In fact, as the weeks and months went on I realized more fully that surely that is the only reason I live. I live to declare to the world that God is alive, and is a worker of miracles, and saved me from death.

My body was hurting. I was taking the maximum quantity permitted of morphine and yet still the pain was great. One thing I have always been frightened of is physical pain. I felt I did not have the capacity to bear severe pain, and it had often crossed my mind that I would not manage it very well. The subject of suffering is a very important issue, and is very difficult to come to terms with. I accept that the world is a painful place to live in and there is suffering everywhere. Rather than asking why we have to suffer, I believe it is more positive to try to see God within the pain. Certainly I experienced God within my suffering, and I was given the strength to cope – even when I was stabbed and the pain was excruciating, I managed to bear it and remain conscious. I believe that the power of God was at work in the midst of the crisis.

On my fifth day in hospital the doctor informed me I could go home in the next few days. I was horrified as I was still being drip fed, and had not yet even been able to get out of bed, or become mobile in any way. The nurse reassured me that I could stay as long as I wanted. The next day I tasted food again. I have never eaten such a delicious baked potato, even though it did not look very appetizing! The following day I was able to move from the restrictions of my bed. The physiotherapist was sent to help me, and gave me confidence to move about and to start walking again.

Soon the day came for me to go. The West London Mission arranged that I should go away for a few weeks' convalescence. The superintendent minister called for me in his car and took me to my flat, where, with the help of my daughters, I collected some belongings. He then drove me to Rickmansworth. I stayed in a home for retired local preachers, where they had a spare room, and it very conveniently fitted my purposes. I was exhausted by the time I arrived, as I had for the first time, since surgery, climbed stairs, packed a case and travelled by car a reasonable distance; that night my body ached and ached.

Now I was pleased to be in a room on my own. I felt safe enough because I was away from the centre of London, and because I felt that there was no way my attacker would know where I was staying. My room was on the ground floor, and I was a little nervous of that fact, until I realized that just outside my window there was a three-foot gap with a long drop down to the basement floor.

Fear was to become my enemy. God had healed me by giving me the gift of forgiveness, from bitterness and revenge, but it was fear that gripped me now, and it emerged in different ways. The first time I got into a car I was afraid that I might have an accident. I felt so vulnerable. Each night I left the main light on as well as the small bedside light and I locked the door. Being a home for retired people, there were emergency bells to ring if I needed help. Sleep evaded me as I was still in pain. I think that after such a major trauma, my body and mind could not cope with another trauma, so I was overprotective towards myself.

More flowers arrived. It was a pity that I had to leave so many flowers at the hospital but the ward was so warm that they were already dying. Letters continued to flood in and by the end of my three-week stay at Rickmansworth, I had received nearly 200 letters and cards.

If I thought I was going to have peace and quiet, then I was mistaken. At least one visitor came to see me each day. So many people wanted and needed to see me, I think just as much to reassure themselves as for my sake. I did enjoy their visits, and was grateful for their kindness. The detective still needed to see me, and Pamela, a counsellor from Victim Support, came and listened to my story. I had not known previously about Victim Support, and was very impressed with the service. I also was impressed by the quality of service from the police. I had not realized how they cared for victims. I found them to be incredibly patient, caring and understanding.

I made tremendous progress during the time at Rickmansworth. I walked round the garden as often as I could, and when visitors were able they escorted me to the town or to the nearby parkland area; slowly, of course. Naturally, I would not dare to venture out on my own at this stage. Even when I was with another person, I was nervous when being approached by any male on his own; I would imagine that he might have a weapon hidden somewhere. But I was able to get out of doors most days, and the colour began to come back to my cheeks. The weather was mostly dry and sunny, even warm enough to sit out, although it was now October.

Only the manager and his wife knew about what had happened to me. I did not want the other residents to be upset or nervous. After a few days, though, it became difficult for me to hide the truth from the other members of staff, because there was so much activity from the police. One day a police photographer came to take photographs of my wounds and I suggested to the manager that the staff should know because they would wonder what was going on. They were horrified and upset when they found out. This is one aspect I found so very difficult to grasp – that people who did not even know me were so upset by it all. The effect it had on some other people was devastating. One member of staff shared with me that she had been raped as a young girl, and I was able to help her come to terms with it. Even in my weakness, God had begun to use my experience to help others without me trying. At this early stage, only weeks after the incident, God was using my pain and suffering to heal others.

One day a minister came to take the morning worship, and I found myself telling him what had happened. He sat and listened, open-mouthed in astonishment. When he learned that this had all happened only a few weeks previously, he could not believe how well I was emotionally, since I was talking about it so rationally. God was already using me to witness to the world the fact that He had saved me and given me life again. The forgiveness was obvious, no words were needed. Forgiveness was very powerful in my mind at this time. It seemed to fill my very being. Each morning we had a short service and always said the Lord's prayer. When we came to the words 'And forgive us our debts, as we also have forgiven our debtors' (Matthew 6:12) I wanted to shout them out. God had filled me with so much forgiveness that it was bursting out of my very soul, overflowing so much that I could not contain it.

As I began to feel a little stronger, I decided to write letters to all the people who might not have known what had happened to me. Of course, it had been reported in the national papers widely but my name had not been disclosed. I suddenly had an overwhelming inner compulsion to pray for my attacker, and I felt I needed to tell the whole world and ask everyone possible to pray along with me. It is difficult to describe this tremendous urge to pray for this man, but these words, spoken to Julian of Norwich by God, seem to fit best:

> I am the ground of your praying. First it is my will that you should have this, then I make it your will too, then I make you ask for it, and you do so. How then should you not have what you pray for?[1]

Just as I was completely and utterly taken over by God when the forgiveness burst out of my soul, the compulsion to pray for this man came in the same way. At those times when God takes over it feels like an explosion coming from deep inside.

I frantically wrote letters to all the people I could think of, urging them to pray for this man. That is all I wrote – 'please pray for him'. When I recall it now, I can still feel the compelling power that was within me, the power which was flowing through me like a channel. It was only months later that I heard how the recipients of these letters had been moved by those words, and I realized that God had been very powerful in this because it was obviously His will. When I was able, I visited as many churches and cathedrals as possible, and left little prayer notes asking people to pray for this unknown man.

Notes

1. Julian of Norwich, *Enfolded in Love*, London, Darton, Longman & Todd, 1980, p. 19.

11

Reconciliation

I now had to learn to trust people again. I found myself realizing my own vulnerability and weakness, and feeling particularly insecure in the company of men. Even with men I knew, I felt nervous that they might suddenly change from their normal calm mood and turn on me. This nervousness only happened when I was alone with a man, being very aware that most men are physically stronger than women. For example, on the day I arrived at Rickmansworth for my convalescence, I experienced this doubt when the manager showed me round the premises. As I found myself in the lift with him alone, my mind panicked for a few seconds, because I would have been trapped if he decided to attack me. All these thoughts were only to be expected, of course, after such a brutal attack.

By the time I left Rickmansworth I was beginning to feel that I could do with time completely on my own. I had received many visitors and spent a lot of time on the telephone. I was not ready at this stage, though, to cope with complete isolation, neither physically or mentally. But I longed for the freedom to be able to do things on my own, to just go out for a walk or to sit in the park, even if just for a short time. But that luxury eluded me. It was not possible because I did not feel safe, and I did not want to take the risk.

My daughters had missed me as they were not able to see very much of me at Rickmansworth – it was a long way to travel, so their visits were restricted to the weekends. My brother, Ray, offered to take me away for a short break, and so I decided to go and stay with Martene for a few days. Ray would then collect me to go off on a short holiday, and then take me to my home. I could not face going to the flat in London to live, as I had only been there for such a short time. I needed to get back to where I felt secure, to my home in Cheshire. Ray arrived. He had driven all the way from Liverpool to collect me. I had only a few belongings – just one suitcase and a bag – and we went to stay near Ross-on-Wye for a few days. I enjoyed the break and was able to relax. By the end of my stay, though, I was beginning to feel tired of moving about, from hospital to convalescence, to Martene's and now for a short break. Whilst I was keen to enjoy the time with my family and appreciated their concern and care, it was unsettling. An added burden was that I was required to keep in close contact with the police. That was a necessity and there was nothing I could do about it. It was a great relief when Ray drove me to my home town.

I was not ready to live on my own at this stage, and so went to stay with a friend nearby who had very kindly offered to look after me for a while. This provided me with the security of company, and I was able to spend some time each day in my own house, which helped me to ease in gradually into living on my own.

After two weeks' stay with my friend I decided I was ready to try sleeping in my own house. This was a major step and I did it. I was very nervous, though. I still needed to keep a small light on at night which, unfortunately, did not help me with my sleep, but I rested and slept lightly and fitfully, although not as well as I would have liked. But I was determined not to give in to my fears.

Now the major step had been taken. I was in my own home once again, and I could begin to feel the security of familiar surroundings. It would take time, and I needed to be patient and wait, while my healing became real. The weeks went by, and I soon found it was time to return to the hospital for a checkup and to see the detective again. I decided to travel alone in an attempt to regain some of my independence. Only weeks before I would not have hesitated or even thought about travelling on my own, I would just do it. Now it was different. I had to learn to regain my confidence. I felt like a child having to learn quite simple tasks. I felt nervous buying my ticket, and although I had experienced the same journey many times before, I approached it with trepidation. For days I thought about it and imagined myself on the train. 'What if I'm the only one in the carriage, and a man gets on who looks scruffy? What if … what if?' ran through my mind. But I was not going to let that stop me. I had made up my mind, and would go on my own. A neighbour gave me a lift to the small country station and the train was on time. I felt vulnerable just standing on the platform. I stepped on, and looked around hesitantly. I noticed there were a few passengers dotted about, so I sat down feeling relieved. More passengers boarded at Crewe and the carriage gradually filled up. Thank goodness, I thought, one hurdle over. The journey soon passed, and I arrived at Euston where I was met by the detective who escorted me to the hospital. I was then taken to meet the Air Ambulance crew and to see the helicopter. Steve Bree (the doctor from HEMS) was there to meet me. He asked me if I remembered it all, and I was able to say yes, although it was blurred. I remembered the dash to the helicopter across the woodland. I remembered the journey, and I remembered the race from the helicopter into the hospital. He was amazed at how well I looked. The detective and I then went on to have lunch together, and then we went to a police station, where we trawled through the statement again.

Travelling home on the train that evening revealed once again that fear would emerge in the most unexpected places. Sitting staring out of the window, watching the day draw to a close as darkness crept upon the countryside, I suddenly realized that the small country station where I would alight would be desolate and deserted, as the station is not staffed in the evening. It would be pitch black, and I would have to cross over the bridge on my own, and then proceed along a passageway. I felt frightened and worried, and felt sure I would panic. My neighbour had said he would come to meet me, but I worried he might not think to walk to the platform and might stay in the car. Then I started to think about how sometimes it is difficult to open the door of the train. I imagined myself to be the only person getting off at this station, that the door would be jammed, and that I would be unable to get off. This feeling of being trapped was quite understandable, after my experience of being held captive in such a savage way. My fears were alleviated, however, and I breathed a sigh of relief, when I saw many people put on coats and lift down baggage as we neared the destination. It was obviously used by people frequently who lived in the area. It was the only evening train direct from Euston which stopped at this particular station. I was reassured to know that I would not be crossing the bridge across the railway line on my own – I would have the company of a handful of others from my carriage alone.

That day provided another major hurdle in my healing. I had travelled to London on my own. Months earlier, before my attack, I would think nothing of such journeys, and had travelled alone all over the world, even to Australia. I was slowly regaining my confidence.

Now that I was living at my own house, it would only be a matter of time before I could lead a normal life again, whatever that is. Life, of course, would never be the same again. Circumstances had totally changed the direction of my life.

Each day I made the effort to walk into town, reluctantly using the road rather than the footpaths I so loved across the park. I knew that one day I would be able to walk along the river again on my own, and I longed for the courage to do that. The courage was there one day, and whilst in the town I thought: 'I've got to do it one day – I'll go back home along the river.' So I proceeded across the park and then along a short stretch of riverbank, which would take me over the locks and then quickly to my house. I was walking along the short stretch of river; there was not a soul in sight. I kept looking round nervously. Then halfway along that stretch I noticed a man coming towards me. He was young and looked a bit unkempt. My heart began to pound, and as he approached closer and closer, it pounded even faster. He went by. I decided that I wasn't ready to walk alone along the riverbank yet. But I had done it once, and I would do it again.

By now, I had made good contact with Russ, and we spent a few evenings together. It seemed incredible that we could meet again and that we could be friends. I never dreamt this would happen. There were many things we wanted to discuss with each other. A most wonderful revelation occurred to me after we spent many hours discussing our relationship, and that was that we had both forgiven each other for the past hurts before this tragic event had brought us together again. God had been working in our lives, and we each had come to terms with life on our own, and felt at peace with it all. How wonderful that God had given us the gift of forgiveness for each other. Now we were meeting again as two new people, and we needed to learn about each other. It is wonderful that God brought us back together to be very special friends through such an incident. I believe the ability to forgive him, and for him to forgive me, is just as powerful as the forgiveness I received for my attacker. This relationship was also of vital importance to me, because it showed me that I was learning to trust again. Russ provided for me a great deal of support at my time of need. He supported me financially, and also provided a listening ear. Over and over again I would repeat the same story about the attack, and he just listened, never needing to offload on me. This was marvellous, and I realized that God had sent him to be used. Russ was willing and open to God's call.

I found some very appropriate words in the book *Life Giving Spirit* by Alwyn Marriage. For me this depicts life for my future, my future with God and my future with Russ. I find these words very powerful.

> It is tempting, when we have been happy with someone, to go back to the same place, or attempt to do the same thing, instead of accepting that the relationship transcends past activities, and may well blossom more beautifully if we go forward into the unknown together. Similarly, with our loving encounters with God, we must be prepared to let go of the gifts we have received in the past, and move on into life in the power of the spirit.[1]

This passage became very real to me, because I realized that we needed to look afresh at who we were, to forget the past and look only to the future. Soon after I was divorced, I decided that my wedding and engagement rings were being wasted lying in the drawer, so I thought of a constructive way to use them. I took them to a jeweller, and asked if they could be melted down to make a cross from the gold. The diamond could go towards the cost of the workmanship. I chose the design and the pattern to be engraved on the front. The jeweller made a beautiful gold cross which I now treasure. The point is that I have a piece of jewellery which symbolizes my commitment to and dependence on God completely. Nobody would ever know that the cross was once my wedding and engagement rings. This cross symbolizes the transformation of my relationship with Russ. Sometimes relationships need to be melted down, and reformed into something completely different, unrecognizable, and with a new purpose and meaning. To consider going back would be out of the question; to consider making two rings again out of the cross would not be right. To go forward means to accept a new and different relationship, built on new foundations.

Russ was kind enough to spend a lot of time with me, helping me with all the practicalities of life. He carried my shopping, gave me lifts (as I had no transport) and accompanied me on walks to some of my favourite places. I was grateful for his company, and for his help.

As part of my healing process, I decided to take up swimming, a most relaxing form of exercise. My first attempt was painful. I expected to be able to swim with the same vigour and speed as I had always done, and I was surprised to find that I had to take it easily and gently. Soon though, I was up to speed, and enjoying myself. Working out at the gym was also helpful. I was given a special programme to follow to strengthen my muscles. I was determined to get myself well again, and the most important thing at this time was to work on my physical healing.

Most of my belongings were still in the flat in London, and I decided to bring them back to my home in Cheshire, since I did not know how long it would be before I was fit for work again. I really felt an uneasiness and restlessness, which I imagined would be eased if I settled in one place for a while. Russ played a major part in all of this. He hired a van, took two days off work, and we drove to our daughter's house to stay for the weekend. Arriving at the flat again, I was reminded that only weeks previously I had arrived there with the removal van to unload, and I had wondered at that time what was in store for me. Never in a million years could I have dreamt that I would be back here so soon, taking all my belongings back to my own home. I could not stop thinking and imagining what would have happened to all my possessions had I not lived! We settled down to the arduous task of packing everything into boxes, and the following day we packed the van, and then drove home. That long and tedious journey, across London and over many miles of motorway, took most of the day. It was a new adventure, one which I had not planned. It was so wonderful to be helped in this way by Russ, as there was no way I could have done it on my own. Once I was surrounded by my belongings I felt even more secure. This was an essential and effective part of my healing.

Early one morning in November I received a phone call from the police to tell me some news. My hopes were raised, as I heard the excitement in the voice of the detective. They had found the attacker of a woman who was raped just three days after me in a nearby location, but it was not the same man who had attacked me. My disappointment regarding this was quite significant, because the police had been running the enquiries side by side, keeping an open mind about whether the attacker was the same. I had felt all along that it would not be the same man, because in my case he attempted to kill me and although the other rape was violent I felt it did not bear the same resemblances. Feelings of jealousy arose, though, and I felt very angry that the police had caught this other man and not my attacker. I felt jealous that the other case could now be dealt with and completed. I was silently screaming for my case to be finalized.

The months were passing by, and it was now January. One of the things that disturbed me most was that of other serious crimes. Only a few miles away from where I live, a young girl was kidnapped whilst riding her bicycle along a country lane, taken in the boot of a car to a house, and raped. Her attacker tried to strangle her, and then dumped her in the road. I was deeply disturbed. My emotions were mixed. I realized that I wanted attention, and I wanted people to see how bad my case was. My mind was shouting out again, saying: 'What about me?' I was jealous because there was a lot of press coverage, and that it was this particular case that blocked mine from being broadcast on the BBC's *Crimewatch* programme in February. I struggled with it, and eventually accepted that this other case needed the help of the public far more urgently than mine, because they had no idea where the house was where the girl had been taken. Other major crimes disturbed me in this way, too, and I could not bring myself to read about them in the newspapers.

Notes

1. Marriage, Alwyn, *Life-Giving Spirit*, London, SPCK, 1989, p. 103.

12

Search for My Attacker

Pamela, the Victim Support Counsellor who had previously helped me, met me at Euston. It was a Sunday afternoon in March, and I was going to her house to stay the night, so that I could be up bright and early, and at the location ready for filming. ITV were planning to show my case on the *Crime Monthly* programme which covers London and the south-east of England, and I was to take part in the action and be interviewed. It was now six months since the rape, and although the police had been confident about locating my attacker because of the good information in hand, they had not yet been successful.

We met at 8 a.m. at the Richmond Arms Hotel the next day. The detective superintendent arrived with one other officer involved in the investigation. At 8.30 a.m. the film crew arrived. We walked to the top of Richmond Hill where I was filmed strolling along looking at the view, that beautiful view of the River Thames which I had seen that day six months earlier; the view that prompted me to change my mind about which way to walk, that led me down the path to meet with that evil deed. Richmond is one of the most luxurious and expensive areas to live and to own property, and we were just across the road from the home of Mick Jagger and Jerry Hall. In the distance we could see Tommy Steele's mansion, a big black and white building almost hidden amongst trees. It was another beautiful day, just as it was on that September day, with a blue sky and white puffy clouds. I was filmed walking down some steps and sitting on a bench. That is where the actress was substituted to act out the reconstruction of the incident.

The detective then drove us to the pub, where some more filming was to take place. This pub was where the suspect is thought to have been seen drinking cream sodas just a few minutes after the crime. It was being used in the reconstruction, in the hope that somebody might remember the man and further clues might be found, if only to eliminate any suspects. The police and television crew gathered – there was quite a crowd by now. It was about 9.30 a.m., and the pub was not open to the public, but was so bustling with film crews and police, that for one moment I was not conscious of the fact. Suddenly I reeled; my hand went to my mouth and I gasped. Shock pierced my soul and my heart pounded. In front of me stood a man, a man whom I recognized all too well. He had walked in through the door and stopped. The face was familiar; the scratch on his face, the scruffy appearance, the clothing and the memory of that image jumped from my subconscious. I thought I was looking into the face of my attacker. I soon realized that this was the actor playing the attacker's role. His likeness was so good, though, that the detective's first reaction was to arrest him! My hopes that the programme would achieve the desired results rose dramatically because of the uncanny likeness of this man to my attacker. Added to that, with the description of the tattoos, I hoped and believed that he must be recognized by someone, and found. The make-up artist then proceeded to paint on his body the tattoos that I had described. The crew were going to film the rape scene in order to show the man taking his clothes off, thus revealing the tattoos on his body.

The detective assured me that this *Crime Monthly* programme reached viewers not only in London but in the provinces. He was confident that it would reach far afield enough to bring some more leads to find this man.

My interview then took place in the pub. The interviewer asked me why I had moved to London, and why I had come to Richmond for a walk. She then asked me how I felt about the attacker. I was able to say that I had forgiven him.

Next, the detective, Pamela and I were to walk along the tow-path, to find the specific location of the incident. Revisiting the scene of the crime six months after the event was a curious experience. I recognized the path, but the surrounding woodland appeared different. It was now spring and the leaves were only just beginning to bud. The scrubby land that had been so full of undergrowth in September was now almost bare. It had all been cut down by the police in their fingertip search for clues, and for the knife which had been discarded. The recent rains had flooded part of the land on which I was brutalized. Nevertheless, the location was recognizable. Yet as I walked along the path, and stood at the spot where the attack began and finished, I felt no emotion. I had come to this place with an open mind, yet for some reason had expected to feel something. I imagined either that I would relive the scene and that the film would re-run in my mind, or that I would be overcome with some emotion. But there was nothing, just a void, a complete detachment from what had happened. I could have been anywhere. The vivid, extreme horror and glory I had witnessed at that time was gone, empty, dead, as if these two extremes could not possibly have happened here. It was hard to believe. No wonder Cecil, the man who rescued me, found it difficult to believe. No wonder the nearby residents were horrified to hear of such an horrendous crime being imposed upon me here. The point is that it *was* different, different in the sense that the event was not happening then. It is the time and events that mean something in life, not the physical place. It is the emotions that are felt and thoughts that are important in life, not the place where they happen.

The days following the visit to the scene and the TV interview were hard. My mind was disturbed, particularly because I had seen the face of the actor portraying my attacker, and I felt something new, a deeper sense of the horror of it all. It had been brought back into the forefront of my mind. I realized that now I was also experiencing it through the eyes of other people, particularly Cecil and others who were at the scene. Now I was experiencing a deep sadness and shock by looking at the event as if I were someone else. How horrific for Cecil to stand and watch helplessly as my attacker plunged that knife into my body in an attempt to kill me. How helpless he must have felt, standing watching me lying on the floor near death's door. I had moved out of myself and away from my own narrow view of it all, into the shoes of these other witnesses, and was able to empathize in some small way.

The burden was heavy, and I realized that I was carrying a weighty cross. I prayed, like Jesus, that this cup might be taken from me, but then felt that would not be right. I needed to carry this load, as I saw it as my duty and responsibility to society and to other women. I was the person who had experienced that attack. I was the person who had some insight into the life of my attacker. The day I felt the burden most heavily was the day the programme was being shown. I decided not to eat that day. I realized that it was right that I carry my cross so heavily on that particular day. My sadness was deep towards my attacker, as I felt such compassion for him and for all the evil in the world.

How wonderful that God gives us the strength to cope. Whilst I was experiencing such a deep sense of sadness, I also grasped the fact that I was given a new strength by God alongside this, a deeper strength just for that day because I had taken on the load and carried it.

The *Crime Monthly* programme produced a very accurate description of the event, and many leads were produced for the police to follow up. None of them, however, led to the arrest of my attacker. It was only months later, when I watched the video of the programme, that I discovered that although the actor looked so like my attacker and played the part in a most convincing manner, what did not become apparent was the fear that was present in the real scene. The actor played the man to be ruthless, which was the truth, but missed out the fact that he was full of fear, and such a sad victim of circumstances. I believe that would be very difficult to portray.

Now, nearly eight months since the attack, I needed to attend the hospital out-patients department for a checkup. Russ wanted to share some time with me at the scene of the crime, and so we combined these two deeds on our visit to London. I, too, wanted to revisit the location, because on my first visit when I went for the *Crime Monthly* programme, the land had been flooded and so I was not able to find the exact location of my attack in the woodland area. I had no reservations about going to London, and in fact felt that I could cope with it on my own by this time. However, it would not be wise to go to Ham Common without an escort; even the police were advised to go in pairs.

The day was warm and sunny, just as it had been many months before. Spring was not in its fullness, but the trees and undergrowth were lush and green. This time we travelled by underground from Euston to Richmond, as I wanted to travel in the same way that I had done those many months earlier. I hoped to be able to establish a further sense of healing, by going through the motions and taking the same route. We arrived at Richmond station, and walked up to the point on Richmond

Hill where I noticed the river and the path running alongside, and then we headed down that path. Walking that same route did bring back memories of the day I first walked there. I looked round as I had done previously, and drank in the beauty and wonder of God's creation. I observed that a number of boats were still moored along the opposite side of the river, as if time had not passed. People were still lazily relaxing on their decks. I began to feel a little hesitant in pursuing this exercise, because any emotion could suddenly emerge and would need to be acknowledged.

We walked on until we reached the place where the path narrowed. I prayed as I walked, because I felt I needed God's strength all around me. Now we were quite close to the spot, and this part of the path was quieter and more deserted again. We found the concrete post that the police used as a marker to indicate where I was stabbed, and stood looking round. Again I felt no emotion, as was the case on my first revisit here. I stopped and stared, gazing once again at the scene. This time, though, I intended to find the two exact places where the man raped me. As we scrambled through the rough terrain, I recalled how this had happened previously. The first spot was only a few feet from the path, but the second place was quite a distance. I remember that in the first spot we were disturbed by a man walking along the path, and so, as he dragged me across to the second place, my trousers were trailing behind me, and my legs were getting scratched as he pulled me through the prickly brambles. Even though in my mind I recalled the incident clearly. I did not feel distressed. We found the exact location where there were some trees, and I found that one particular tree, through which shone the great light. To symbolize new life, growth and healing, I planted two small conifers at that second place. It was here that I had the vision of Christ. It was here those few months before that I believe God touched that man that day, and so it was here that I needed to mark the place with something that would speak of that important part of my experience. As I looked up to the sky through that same tree, I remembered the way I had felt that day. It looked just the same. We prayed for my attacker, for the police and for ourselves. We prayed that the planting of the trees would symbolize the planting of the Word of God and of new life. I thought it appropriate that here was a place of woodland, near the river, which would provide life-giving water for the growth of the trees.

The next day I visited the hospital. I was feeling well and it showed. The doctor on duty examined me and his only comment to me was 'You're incredible!' I did not have to say much, rather just present myself, and I knew that only in God's power could I be healed in such a wonderful and mighty way. The doctor confirmed to me that mine was a case where the Air Ambulance really did save my life. I was so pleased to be there, and to witness to the doctor what they had done for me. I think I reassured the doctor that day, and helped him to feel that his job was worth all the effort. He was looking at a miracle.

13

Love

To be able to love as God loves us is one of the greatest challenges for anyone. Such pure and perfect love seems beyond the realms of most individuals, yet the miracle is that it can be possible.

My family showed unconditional love in abundance. My mother never once denied me love, no matter what I did. I did not have to earn love, and that provided a wonderfully reassuring security, and probably helped me really to understand how God loves every one of us unconditionally. Realistically, I do understand that the love my mother showed me was not perfect, because she was human. But for many people their experience of love is conditional, lacking and deformed. It is sad that so many children are not shown love at all. People who have not experienced human love must find it difficult to realize the love of God, but once experienced, it is a remarkable revelation.

To love is to make oneself vulnerable, because loving involves sacrifice and giving. Love may be gentle and kind, but real love is not sloppy and sentimental. Love is courageous and creative, rather than weak and feeble. Pure love is being able to accept another individual as they are, accepting all their faults and difficulties, and allowing them to be themselves without judgement. It involves looking beyond the surface, beneath the skin, and seeing the potential of the other. Love is surely a gift from God, born of Him. One who loves is borne on wings, and is free and unrestricted as it brings liberation. Love allows us to go beyond the boundaries that we make for ourselves and which imprison us. When a person loves, they become rich, creative and productive. Love's energy and power are much greater than hate's. It is a strong force which burns like a fire within. Pure love never seeks its own ends, and gives without expecting to receive anything in return.

For most of our lives we experience a love towards others which is only partial because we inhibit ourselves, not daring to risk this dynamic force which enables us to be vulnerable. We dare not risk the pain and hurt we may experience. But if we give ourselves fully, and love completely, the reward produces an exuberant freedom. Jesus taught His disciples to love above all else, and this is of paramount importance in His teaching.

In order to love others, we must learn to love ourselves. A sad reflection of the teaching of the Church, is that to love oneself is omitted all too often, leaving people depleted, worn out, trying to love others from a sense of duty.

When we read in the first letter of John that we should love one another, John is telling the people not to be like Cain who murdered his brother (2:11–12). If I had been in the congregation he was addressing, I might have been quite offended by his message. I would imagine that the people he was talking to were quite ordinary people, and not criminals. I believe that he was referring to everyone, people like you and me who quarrel with each other over minor things. The message imparted here, I believe, is that not to love, or to take the stand of passive neutrality, is to destroy, and when we do not love as Christ loves, we are in fact using a weapon just as effective as any other murder weapon. That sounds very harsh, but perhaps John needed to shock his congregation. Lack of love means that relationships and characters are destroyed. Hate, bitterness and unforgiveness are murderous weapons, and the appalling fact is that all too often this is experienced within the established Church. Society expects this sort of behaviour in the secular world, particularly in business where the power game is so important, and everyone is so determined to have their own way to achieve their own goals. Individuals compete against individuals, as do rival companies; countries fight to possess land. Jesus taught us to give without counting the cost, and to risk losing our possessions. I believe we have a responsibility to witness to the world that love is possible in the truest sense, and that must come by example.

It is difficult to know how to love in the way that Jesus loved and still loves. Because we are human we are not perfect, but the love of Jesus is perfect. Yet love does not plead impossibility. I believe that with the advent of the New Covenant, Jesus invites us to share in the connection of marriage between heaven and earth. Our part is to love one another as Jesus loves us. In return we receive the Spirit of God, alive, flowing through us and being channelled through us. Perfect love means not manipulating others, but rather laying down ourselves and giving our true selves to one another. Perfect love means a total giving, and not counting the cost.

We cannot possibly love like Jesus in our own strength, but it is possible if we have faith in Him. As we love Jesus, the energy and power which is in Him begins working in our lives. As God's love comes alive in us, we will be able to share it with one another. In fact, we will not be able to hold back the flow as the dam bursts.

One of the greatest I AM sayings of Jesus is 'I am the true vine' (John 15:1). To connect with the life-giving love of Jesus enables us to love. If we dwell in Jesus, His life will flow through us and we will bear much fruit. The grapes grow as the sap flows along the vines, and in the same way we will bear fruit, as the love is poured into and through us, as long as we allow this to happen. To receive this love from God is of vital importance. Love is accepting a gift and loving the giver, not the gift, and so, essentially, loving God.

I believe that it is necessary to break down many of the barriers that are set up by organizations like the Church, which inhibit the flow of love. Jesus broke the rules of the day, because He realized that relationships are more important than rules. Rules can be helpful at times, but can also be alarmingly inhibiting. Loving is going one step further than the law – it is going deeper, being vulnerable. Love means behaving in a way that is demanding. Jesus mixed with tax collectors, sinners, harlots and Samaritans. That was not acceptable to the Jewish tradition of the day; in fact, it was an outrage. If Jesus was here now He would most probably be found in the pubs, the betting shops and at car-boot sales! Love breaks all the rules.

Eddie Askew wrote a meditation in his book *Breaking the Rules* which sums this up neatly:

Lord, take it easy, please,
Slow down, I can't catch up with you.
Can't find the courage to ignore convention.
Break the mould.
The only thing that holds my life together
is the rules I make.
That's how I know just where I am,
safe in a shaky scaffolding
or do-it-yourself certainty.
Built, bit by bit,
from a prepacked kit of orthodoxy.
Individually designed, they say,
but made to sell in thousands.
Market researched. Acceptable to all.

Matching the decor,
and coming with a lifelong guarantee
against reality breaking in.
I know just whom to like,
whom to invite to dinner, who's acceptable.
And who is better kept at arm's length.
And seeing you behave
as though the rules don't matter,
frightens me.
Makes me tremble,
watching you undo the bolts
that dislocate the framework of my life.
Leaving the house I've built
vulnerable to the first wolf that comes along.
And others feel just as uncertain Lord,
I wish you'd realize that.
They're happier too,
if they are able to predict
just what you'll do or say.
More sensible all round.
Of course there'll always be some folk outside,
excluded by my rules.
Unfortunate. But then, that's life.
And suddenly, I notice, with unease,
you standing with them,
outside the boundary wire of my concern.
Not asking that they be admitted to my world,
but offering me the chance
to leave my warm cocoon,
thermostatically controlled by selfishness,
and take my place with them,
and you.

At risk in real relationships,
where love, not law, defines what I should do.[1]

Yet the love of God is constantly beaming down on everyone, even those people who do not want to receive His amazing and magnificent gift. Nothing can stop the flow of love from God.

David Runcorn, in his book *Touch Wood*, writes: 'The cross of Jesus is a gift of divine love to people who have no way of receiving it. More than that, God's love is given to those who violently reject it.'[2]

I was sitting in church one Sunday only weeks after my attack when the minister spoke about us all being equal in the eyes of God. Suddenly the concept struck me that I am not superior to the man who raped me and tried to kill me. This equality of all human beings had been presented to me all my life, and I understood it to be true, yet somehow, at that moment, I knew it in a deeper way. During the service we sang a hymn which suggested that I place into the hands of God anything I felt I could not do on my own, and which challenged me to love the people that God would especially love. Tears filled my eyes at this point: tears of compassion for this man whom I realized that God loved just as much as me, and that He wanted to love in a very special way.

My experience of that horrific attack brought me to realize that it is possible at times to love as God loves. I glimpsed for a few moments of my life, a few moments in time and eternity, that pure and perfect love. I had known it on the day when I was physically with my attacker and I was conscious of it now; that love which enables a person to see another through the eyes of God and love in the way He loves, with compassion. I believe that this is how, in that same way, I could forgive him. Never before, and I doubt if ever again, will I experience such an awareness of perfect love.

Our psyche is very complicated. The following passage by Gerard Hughes challenged me to see that although the man who attacked me had done this most horrific thing, he was also capable of doing amazingly wonderful things. It also brought me to realize that even the most saintly person is capable of committing horrific acts. The choice is our own, but the fact remains that we are all capable of the extremes.

> If we really could see into the depths of ourselves and into our subconscious and unconscious minds, we would recognize in ourselves all the characteristics of the demoniac and this would terrify us, but we would see also other qualities which would delight us. There is no crime, no perversion, no cruelty ever practised of which we are not capable, but there is no heroism, selflessness or love which is beyond our potential. Because we are afraid of looking at the evil possibilities in us, we fail also to see our true greatness.[3]

Subsequently I attended a Bible study. The person who was leading that evening had no idea that I was going to attend. The theme for that evening was 'love your enemy'. He read the passage to which I referred earlier from the first letter of John and then asked us to imagine being in a situation whereby someone was threatening our lives. I did not have to use my imagination! He then challenged us to think about our reactions, to see whether we could wash the feet of the attackers, even though they might kill us afterwards. God was really challenging me here.

My attacker was a desperate man in a great deal of need, but to love this man in the way God was challenging me now was to take it to another level. It felt like an outrage, and was just as demanding as forgiving. The only way anyone can love in this way is by accepting the love of God, and allowing that love to flow through to the other person. Nothing like this can be done in our own strength alone. I now saw this man as an equal human being, someone to be valued, loved and cherished. Maybe that man had never been loved in his life. One misconception that many people to whom I have spoken have is that our relationship with God depends upon our own goodness. This is a false notion – our relationship with God does not depend on our goodness, but rather on God's love for us.

With the love of God we have no enemies, because if we love, nobody is our enemy. There are few people who can be so transparent that God's love shines through them to love the unwanted, the poor, the smelly, the rejected, the hated and even those who trespass against them. Mother Teresa is one. The example of Mother Teresa here is very powerful, and I quote from a book of her sayings compiled by Malcolm Muggeridge, called *Something Beautiful for God*.

> I do not agree with the big way of doing things. To us what matters is an individual. To get to love the person we must come in close contact with him. If we wait till we get the numbers, then we will be lost in the numbers. And we will never be able to show that love and respect for the person. I believe in person to person; every person is Christ for me, and since there is only one Jesus, that person is only one person in the world for me at that moment.[4]

God's love is given freely by grace, but it is costly. The love of God cannot be separated from the cross and I believe we are all taken to the cross in some way in our own sufferings. Each time I share my story, and tell of the miracle in my life, it costs me the agony of reliving the horror. Each time I express to others or think about that immeasurable love of God for all people, I have to bear the pain of my own cross, and enter into the horror, the agony of that day. It is as if I cannot see or know extreme love without seeing extreme hell. It is a heaven-and-hell experience, where my mind is taken into the depths of extremes; so extreme that it becomes unbearable.

Notes

1. Askew, Eddie, *Breaking the Rules*, Middlesex, The Leprosy Mission International, 1992, p. 7.
2. Runcorn, David, *Touch Wood*, London, Darton, Longman & Todd, 1992, p. 24.
3. Hughes, Gerard, *God of Surprises*, London, Darton, Longman & Todd, 1991, p. 28.
4. Muggeridge, Malcolm, *Something Beautiful for God*, London, Collins/Fontana Books, 1971, p. 118.

14

Friday at Three – Suffering and the Cross

It was Good Friday. The world was at work. I prayed, silently, for him. Scores of shoppers crushed into the supermarkets and stuffed their trolleys to overflowing. I lit a candle. It was ten to three.

I went out and walked by the river. I passed two fishermen. The water was still and silent.

Pain surged through my body: pain, real pain, in the place where I was stabbed. I was living through that awful stabbing episode again. It was now 3.15 p.m.

I stopped in my tracks and caught my breath. What was this mysterious thing happening to me? How was it that I felt the pain again in such a real way? Would I have to suffer this pain for others, in order to pray in a deep and meaningful way? Slowly it dawned on me that the exact timing of all the events that had happened to me were of incredible significance. Today, on Good Friday, I was reliving in a symbolic way the chapter of my life on that memorable day in September. What I had failed to realize earlier was that the incident happened on a Friday at around 3 p.m., the time when Jesus died on the cross. I suddenly saw it all in a new light. I had been taken to the cross, yet it was mystery. I wondered how these remarkable things could be happening to me after such a passage of time. I pondered on the fact that I could be connecting with the experience of Jesus on the cross, both on that Friday in September and on this Good

Friday. Scanning the passage of time and eternity, I began to see that timelessness was the clue. Rather than thinking of the cross in the limited dimension of time and space, I began to understand it in a new way, cutting into time, as if time did not exist. The cross was there at one place and time in history, but it is affecting today. It is a continuous, ongoing, never-ending process, scanning the whole of time, from beginning to end, and I was joining in that dialogue or inter-connectedness with Jesus. I was and am part of the story, intertwined, in the universal web of mystery, holding hands in consolidation with the past, present and future, entering into that timelessness.

On this Good Friday I was entering once again into the pain of the cross, and I believe that God did not want me to forget that pain. It was symbolic of the suffering of the world and enabled me to pray in an intense and meaningful way. It is important to remember that we cannot avoid the cross: we have to face it and go through it. It is only when we have dared to face the cross that we can experience the resurrection. There can be no resurrection without suffering and death, no new life without first dying to the old life.

Peter Abelard had a lifelong struggle on the subject of suffering, and he wrote these words after finding a rabbit suffering in a poacher's trap. He gently released the rabbit and held it in his arms. The rabbit died.

> It was the last confiding thrust that broke Abelard's heart. 'Thibault,' he said, 'do you think there is a God at all? Whatever has come to me, I earned it. But what did this one do?' Thibault nodded.
>
> 'I know,' he said. 'Only – I think God is in it too.'
>
> 'In it? Do you mean that it makes Him suffer, the way it does us?'

Again Thibault nodded.

'Then why doesn't he stop it?'

'I don't know,' said Thibault. 'Unless – unless it's like the Prodigal Son. I suppose the father could have kept him at home against his will. But what would have been the use? All this,' he stroked the limp body, 'is because of us. But all the time God suffers. More than we do.'

Abelard looked at him, perplexed.

'Thibault, do you mean Calvary?'

Thibault shook his head.

'That was only a piece of it – the piece we saw – in time. Like that.' He pointed to a fallen tree beside them, sawn through the middle.

'That dark ring there, it goes up and down the whole length of the tree. But you only see it where it is cut across. That is what Christ's life was; the bit of God that we saw. And we think God is like that because Christ was like that, kind and forgiving sins and healing people. We think that God is like that for ever, because it happened once, with Christ. But not the pain. Not the agony at the last. We think that stopped.'

'Then Thibault,' Abelard said slowly, 'you think that all this,' he looked down at the little quiet body in his arms, 'all the pain of the world, was Christ's cross?'

'God's cross,' said Thibault. 'And it goes on.'[1]

After reading this passage, it became clear to me that what I had experienced was something like this analogy of the tree trunk. At one moment in my history, I had seen and glimpsed the cross in a very real way. More than that, I had shared in a profound way the suffering, captivity, dying and then resurrection with Christ. It appeared as a cameo to me, or like a still photograph at that one moment. The story of the gospel and particularly the cross is continuing today.

Reflection upon this experience caused me to understand a number of things. First, I recognized my vulnerability and powerlessness. As soon as I was attacked I became passive, I was not in control, and therefore I was sharing in the passion of Christ. For most of Jesus' ministry He was active and in control, but as soon as He was captured things were being imposed upon Him: this is the meaning of the passion. Just as Jesus was captured, so was I.

Then I experienced abuse, of the ultimate sort for a woman. The exact nature of the abuse was different, in that I was raped, but it was ultimate in the sense that nothing worse could be done to a woman. My attacker had no respect for me, and I was treated inhumanely. My clothes were stripped from me, torn in two and I was pushed and shoved, violated and abused. Jesus was stripped of His clothes, He was pushed and shoved from one place to another. Both of my hands were cut and my stab wound was through my body on my right side. Some pictures of Jesus on the cross show the wound in His side to be in exactly the same position as mine. My tongue was also split. There was blood on my face, hands and body. When I lay on the ground after being stabbed, I lay in a position as if on a cross with my arms not fully extended, but nevertheless in a similar, horizontal position. This is the way I had been laid down by my rescuer. Then, at the moment which I understood to be the moments before death, I spoke words of forgiveness for my attacker. I experienced the passion of Christ in these ways, I was captured, abused, violated, almost died, went into the depths of hell, and at the same time saw the glory of the risen Christ and I was raised again to new life. That is what it is all about, being given new life. The resurrection of Jesus is to assure us that in Him we can be raised to new life.

It was whilst I was attending a conference in Llandudno that I first understood fully the meaning of the passion. The minister who was leading the conference explained that suffering means being passive and being in the hands of other people's actions. A person enters into passion when they are at the receiving end of what others are doing.

Surely the things that I experienced are not a coincidence? Yet what is the meaning of this? Was I being Christ for my attacker? Was I at one and the same time experiencing looking upon the cross and seeing the risen Christ and yet also being Christ to another? A friend, Joan, believes that just as with Christ, who was wounded for our transgressions, and whose wounds heal us (Isaiah 53:5), we will be used in the same way; by our wounds others will be healed.

> Whenever and whatever we read of Christ in the gospel, we are also reading our own self-portrait, for Christ is what we are called to become. 'God became man' as one of the early Fathers of the Church put it, 'so that man might become God.' ... for to be another Christ is the meaning of our existence.[2]

Throughout history people have understood that through suffering we become Christ to others.

I read that Geoffrey Studdart Kennedy was an army chaplain in the First World War. He wrote these words:

> On June 7th 1917, I was running to our lines half mad with fright, though running in the right direction, thank God, through what had been once a wooded copse. It was being heavily shelled. As I ran, I stumbled and fell over something. I stopped to see what it was. It was an undersized,

underfed German boy with a wound in his stomach and a hole in his head. I remember muttering, 'You poor little devil, what had you got to do with it? Not much great blond Prussian about you.' Then came light. It may have been pure imagination, but that does not mean that it was not also reality, for what is called imagination is often the road to reality. It seemed to me that the boy disappeared and in his place there lay the Christ upon his cross, and cried 'inasmuch as ye have done it unto the least of these my little ones ye have done it unto me.' From that moment on I never saw a battlefield as anything but a crucifix. From that moment on I have never seen the world as anything but a crucifix.[3]

Again, this shared experience of the cross is clearly depicted by Elie Wiesel.

One day when we came back from work, we saw three gallows rearing up in the assembly place, three black crows. Roll call. SS all around us, machine guns trained, the traditional ceremony. Three victims in chains and one of them, the little servant, the sad-eyed angel.
The SS seemed more pre-occupied, more disturbed than usual. To hang a young boy in front of hundreds of spectators was no light matter. The head of the camp read the verdict. All eyes were on the child. He was lividly pale, almost calm, biting his lips. The gallows threw its shadow over him.
The three victims mounted together on to the chairs.
The three necks were placed at the same moment within the nooses.
'Where is God? Where is He?' someone behind me asked.

> At a sign from the head of the camp, the three chairs tipped over.
> Total silence throughout the camp. On the horizon the sun was setting.
> 'Bare your heads,' yelled the head of the camp. His voice was raucous. We were weeping.
> 'Cover your heads.'
> Then the march past began. The two adults were no longer alive. Their tongues hung swollen, blue-tinged.
> But the third rope was still moving, being so light, the child was still alive.
> For more than half an hour he stayed there, struggling between life and death, dying in slow agony under our eyes. And we had to look him full in the face. He was still alive when I passed in front of him. His tongue was still red, his eyes were not yet glazed.
> Behind me I heard the same man asking 'Where is God now?'
> And I heard a voice within me answer him 'Where is He? Here he is – He is hanging here on this gallows.'[4]

It may be the experience of grief or the loss of a loved one, it may be the pain and agony of loneliness. It may be the suffering of depression or a lifelong physical illness. Whatever it may be, it can be possible for us to see we are holding the hand of Jesus, and we are suffering and dying on that cross with Him. Jesus is taking us along that path, the path He trod, the path of the passion. For me that path to the cross was the devastating experience.

My attacker stripped me of everything possible in this life. He wanted to use my body, he took my money, and he wanted my life. He could not have taken more. Yet I knew the only way was to give him all that he asked. In fact, I had no choice, but still if he was so desperate to have all these things, then all I could do was to give them to him. Even to give him my life did not mean that he would own me, because I belong to God, and my death would have meant moving on to the beginning of my life in another world. My attacker could not win.

Notes

1. Abelard, Peter, *The Reprint Society*, 1950, pp. 268–70.
2. Hughes, Gerard, *op. cit.*, p. 113.
3. Quoted in *Lord of the Journey, a Reader in Christian Spirituality*, compiled and edited by Roger Pooley and Philip Seddon, London, Collins, 1986, p. 132.
4. Wiesel, Elie, *Night*, London, Penguin, 1981, p. 73.

15

Life After Rape

Life will never be the same again. Because I crossed over the circumference, beyond, into the next world, but then lived, I am experiencing a sort of separateness from the world, an existential aloneness. This theory is aptly expressed by D. H. Lawrence in his book *Women in Love*, when Birkin is explaining his understanding of love to Gudrun:

> At the very last, one is alone, beyond the influence of love. There is a real impersonal me, that is beyond love, beyond emotional relationship ... The root is beyond love, a naked kind of isolation, an isolated me, that does not meet and mingle, and never can.[1]

The paradox is that whilst I am experiencing a separateness or disconnectedness to the world, at the same time I am aware of a deep connection to all things, creation and humanity, and a sense of unity in all the earth, as if everything is joined together, holding hands, united. We are all unique within the complex order of things. St Paul said that he could not wait to get to heaven, and this is how I feel, because I have had a taste and seen a glimpse of the next world, and so believe I know how wonderful it is going to be. The poem 'The Darkling Thrush' by Thomas Hardy speaks in a small way of this concept. In this poem only the thrush has seen something, some 'blessed hope', that no one else has seen or understands.

The difficulty I have had to face and accept is that not many people understand the fact that I am so alone in my experience. When I moved to my home in Cheshire, one of the priorities to enable my healing was to find a counsellor. Victim Support provided this most essential service and so Christina, a very special person, was able to travel alongside me and empathize with me on my journey. Ultimately, though, the journey is mine and mine alone. I feel irritated when people group victims together, as if all their experiences have been the same. This happens when people suggest that they know someone who had an experience like mine. I can only say that they are mistaken. No one has had my experience; it is different from everybody else's. I have come to realize that every person's experience is unique, no matter how simple or profound. I hope that this will help me to help others, in the sense that I may not make assumptions about others, that I know where they have been, when in fact I have not been along their own particular path. I may choose to be taken with them if they wish to share with me, and if I am able to walk with them on their journey, but at the outset I cannot say I have been there.

Rarely do people experience what is 'beyond the veil' and in the next world. Once along that road it is impossible to return. I believe the result is a heightened state of awareness of the unique self. As we become more and more self-aware, we become more aware of our individuality. We then have less need to cling to others, but rather are content to stand on our own with God.

I love the story *The Velveteen Rabbit* written by Margery Williams. This quotation puts into words the profound truth of becoming real. The two nursery toys, the Skin Horse and the Rabbit are talking:

> 'Does it hurt?' asked the Rabbit.
>
> 'Sometimes,' said the Skin Horse, for he was always truthful. 'When you are real, you don't mind being hurt.'
>
> 'Does it happen all at once, like being wound up,' he asked, 'or bit by bit?'
>
> 'It doesn't happen all at once,' said the Skin Horse. 'You become. It takes a long time. That's why it doesn't often happen to people who break easily, or have sharp edges, or who have to be carefully kept. Generally, by the time you are Real, most of your hair has been loved off, and your eyes drop out and you get loose in the joints and very shabby. But these things don't matter at all, because once you are Real you can't be ugly, except to people who don't understand.'[2]

There really are no words to describe so much of my inner feelings, and I have often wondered what it would be like if there were no words and no language, but only feelings, pictures and memories. One example of trying to grasp this concept can be found in the Bible, when Jesus used the images of the Lamb of God and the Good Shepherd. In some languages there are no words for lamb or shepherd, because they do not have sheep or lambs in their culture.

On holiday in Malta, I decided to attend church – it was Pentecost. I was happy to find an empty church, just to sit and pray. Once inside the beautiful Roman Catholic church, it became obvious that a service was taking place. I stood at the back, just inside the doorway, not wanting to disturb the people worshipping. As my eyes scanned the scene, I became aware of its great beauty; it was decorated with ornate carvings, exquisite paintings and statues, and rich and radiant colours surrounded me. The priest was speaking to the people. There were candles and bells, it was extremely beautiful and I felt the presence of God in there. After a while it became obvious that, even though the service was held in the Maltese language, I was able to understand the words. The Lord's prayer was spoken, they all shared the peace together, and sang the 23rd Psalm, 'The Lord's my shepherd' whilst Communion took place. It was during this Psalm that I was aware of the words 'He restores my soul ... you anoint my head with oil ... my cup overflows' in a most powerful way. I felt a sense of what must have happened on that day of Pentecost 2000 years ago, and I also understood that we do not always have to have the words in our own language to explain whatever is on our heart, but we can communicate in many other ways.

I have been astounded by the way I have been provided with all the material things necessary. I could not have believed that I could live on such a small amount of money, and I have never been short of anything. I had only spent three weeks in my new post in London and I had to let that go, not knowing when I would be ready to take on responsibility for a full-time job again. Russ provided so much help and support, for example, helping me with shopping, food and clothes. I had in the past been very sceptical of people who told of how God provided in times of need, and when I heard stories of people receiving money in envelopes through the letter box I tended to think they were exaggerating. However, it has happened to me, and I am eternally grateful to the people who have given in this way. I believe that God is not only concerned with our basic needs, but also with what I consider luxuries. I own a very good, special watch. I never take it off, even when I go swimming. One day, it stopped and I took it to the jewellers for repair. They told me it would cost £100, which seemed to be rather a high price. I thought it most probably very extravagant and considered discarding it and buying another for much less, but I decided to go ahead with the repair even though I did not have the money, trusting that I would be able to pay when the watch was ready. Two weeks later I went out for the day with a friend. Late in the afternoon, she dropped me off at my house and as she did so she handed me an envelope. When I opened the envelope there was £100. Five minutes later the telephone rang and it was the jeweller informing me that my watch was ready.

Another incident happened during a very cold spell one Christmas when my small electric fan heater, which I use in my bedroom, broke down and was irreparable. A friend called to see me with a Christmas card and when I opened it, there was a £20 note tucked inside. This particular friend had not previously given me a present or money for Christmas. When I went to buy a new fan heater, similar to the one I had, it cost just £20. These incidents, I believe, are the hand of God at work in my life. Not only was I given enough, I feel that I was thoroughly spoiled because I was given two holidays, one in Malta and one in Madeira, during the summer of my convalescence.

You cannot give more than God will provide, and I have found that even though I have had very little money to live on, if and when I have been generous with that small amount, more has poured into the pot. One such incident relating to this is the fact that I made an audio tape of my story, of which I made copies and gave to whoever I felt it would help. I have never charged for these tapes, not even the cost of a blank tape, but as soon as I gave some away, I would receive some money to buy some more blank tapes. God has shown me in this special way that I will never be in want and that everything will be provided. I have also had to learn to let go of so many things in my life during the past few years, and ultimately the challenge was to let go of my life itself.

In Luke we read the story of the rich man who came to Jesus and asked 'What must I do to inherit eternal life?' (18:18–28). The man said that he had kept all the commandments and had done since he was a boy. Jesus, however, saw that he lacked one thing and challenged him to sell all his possessions, give them to the poor and follow Him. The man could not bring himself to do this. The man had kept all the rules, so he thought, by obeying the law. In asking him to dispose of his fortune, Jesus was trying to bring him to the point where he could put his trust in God and not in his own wealth and achievements.

There is nothing wrong in owning possessions, but if our possessions become a god and we depend on them for our happiness, then we will be disappointed. If a person owns great wealth, and understands it all to be a great gift to be used, then that person will be free from the imprisonment of worrying about losing it. Ultimately, the rich man could not do what Jesus asked. He owned lots of money and other possessions, and he loved them more than he loved people or God. He loved himself more than he loved others.

In the past few years I have been challenged by God to let go of many aspects of my life. Firstly, God taught me that ambition and status were of no consequence. Indeed, Jesus himself did not put Himself above God but sought equality. I wanted to serve God and felt it was right to follow that call. When I applied for the ordained ministry it meant leaving behind all that I had ever worked for: my house, my career and my car. I also had to come to terms with leaving all my friends behind. It seems that God was challenging me to give up everything. I could not think of anything else that I might have to give up, but I was mistaken – when my offer for the ministry was not accepted, it seems that God was asking me to let go of that as well. I wondered if my motive for wanting to be a minister was ambition. After that option had slipped out of my grasp, I thought that nothing else could be asked of me. I accepted the situation and was prepared to let go of everything, yes, everything. I prayed to God that I would give my all. I soon found that I was mistaken about the fact that there was nothing else that God might ask. It did not occur to me until weeks after the attack that there was one more thing that I may have to give up and that was my life, my physical life on earth.

I had no choice when I came face to face with death but to accept the plight in which I found myself. Even though I held on to just such a tiny thread of hope that I might escape, I was ready to die and did not fight death, but calmly abandoned myself into the hands of it. This calm acceptance was almost a no-choice place to be. There was no point in fighting. Only later did I realize that I had been challenged to let go of my life. God is the giver of all gifts, and even though I thought I would have to give up most of my possessions and even my life, all was given back to me. Now I can enjoy all these things, knowing that they are a gift from Him.

I believe I helped to build up a certain amount of trust with my attacker. He soon realized that I was going to do as he asked, and I was not going to scream and shout or fight him. I believe this action may have been foreign to him, but it was the only way that I had any hope of surviving. It was as if he was desperately looking for a friend, and in some ways I was fulfilling that role. In the only way I knew possible, I was befriending him as I believed that Christ would have done. I did not want to do this man any harm. My weapon was not a dagger like his: my weapon is love. It was not my job to fight him. All I could do was to see him as Christ would see him, a person in great need.

It's interesting in the story of the rich man that Jesus did not run after him. He did not give him another chance; not that day, anyway. He let him walk away. The man was very sad indeed, with lots of money and possessions, but without that great treasure in heaven which money cannot buy. So I found that amazing tension, that when we are prepared to give up whatever it is we have, for some strange reason it is returned and in abundance. If we give in order to receive, then this concept does not work, but if we give from the heart, then God showers us with His abundant gifts.

Notes

1. Lawrence, D. H., *Women in Love*, London, Penguin, 1989, pp. 207–208.
2. Williams, Margery, *The Velveteen Rabbit*, New York, Knopf, 1984.

16

Cliff Experience

Staring out of the car window, looking over the landscape, scattered with thousands of people, I was exhausted but happy. The massive marquees, erected proudly, housed thousands for the day. I reflected and knew that what had brought me here was that God wanted me to come and study here at Cliff College. It was bank holiday Monday, May 1995, on the Celebration weekend, and this was a special day for me and many others. The day had seen some torrential rain, which had poured on to the tents, and flooded the grounds of this most beautiful place. Just as the rain had poured down, that much needed water for the dry land to drink, for the trees and greenery to flourish, the Word of God had been pouring out upon the people, who had come to receive and to hear what He had to say.

Now, at the end of the day, the sun could just be glimpsed through the clouds and I was sitting in the car with Russ, away from the crowds, staring at the Derbyshire hills. It was like looking at a picture, a picture that had been painted vividly with bright colours. It reminded me of the Pre-Raphaelite paintings 'April Love' by Arthur Hughes, a picture of a young girl by a tree, with every ivy leaf on the tree trunk painted clearly, and with masses of pink petals lying on the ground, and the one by Sir John Everett Millais entitled 'Autumn Leaves', with that great pile of leaves, every one intricately and painstakingly painted in realistic colours. This scene looked just as vivid: the college with its grey stone walls; the green hills in the background; and the massive white marquees that had been used for the meetings for people to hear the Word of God spoken and to sing praises to Him. The sky was mostly grey, but with glimpses of blue just breaking through. Hordes of people, like colonies of ants, were milling around, gathering their belongings, meeting others ready to go home and having conversations with long-lost friends. Many people who had brought their own small tents to sleep in for the weekend were packing up ready to go home, emptying their rubbish into the bins, rolling up sleeping bags and stuffing everything into the boots of their cars. Children were running around, playing, screaming, although, I, being inside the car, with its tightly shut doors and windows could not hear the sounds echoing in the countryside. What I could hear was God speaking to me clearly, saying that my next step would be to spend a year here. I felt it in my bones. It would serve me well for a number of reasons: first, it would help me to get back into the speed of life within a safe environment; second, I felt it would help me when candidating again for the ministry, for that is what I planned to do; and third, whatever my next step would be, the qualification would come in useful. Even though the day had experienced rain and more rain, there was joy in my heart. With wet feet and warm hearts we travelled home.

I pondered on my decision to spend a year at Cliff College, studying for the Certificate in Biblical and Evangelistic Ministry. I was only too well aware that I might find life a little difficult living in a community because I am such an independent person. Still, I considered it would be a good experience for me, and good discipline to attempt this task. I thought that whatever the benefits would be, they would far outweigh any difficulties.

The day came in September 1995 when I set out on my

journey to Cliff. It was the beginning of a new phase in my life, a transition into a new chapter, exciting yet unsettling. It was both a physical journey and a spiritual journey. I packed some belongings into the car, and set off to drive through the Cheshire countryside, and then into Derbyshire. The drive was beautiful, and took me over the road commonly known as the 'Cat and Fiddle', a windy country road, one of the highest spots in England, and which has a pub by that name at its highest point. This road is prone to fog in the winter, but in the summer months and with a clear sky has the advantage of tremendous views. Then it's down into the valley, through Buxton where the road runs alongside a river, with trees on either side and thence into Bakewell. Once through Bakewell, dotted with white-walled and stone cottages, wearing colourful clematis, ivy or – in the autumn – the rich colours of copper beech leaves, it is only a short distance to Calver, the small village where the college is situated.

On arrival I was met by some second-year students, who helped to carry my bags up to my room. Thirty huge stone steps had to be negotiated before we got to the door of the building, then another two flights of stairs and along the corridor to my room. I was pleased with the room I had been allocated. It was right at the end of a wing, so I reckoned that I would be safe from lots of passing traffic and noisy students. The room was quite big compared with some of the others in the corridor, and again I felt thankful for that, because I could enjoy a bit of space. I opened the window, which looked out on to the back of the grounds, and there was a tree and greenery just outside. I imagined that the single bed, bookcase, desk, chest of drawers and wardrobe which furnished the room would be enough to house my belongings.

Once I had moved all my belongings into my room, I went down to the hall to meet the other new students arriving. I felt a bit nervous, not knowing what to expect, and I suppose most of the others felt nervous too. After a meeting which was engineered to introduce all the staff, and to explain the rules of the college, we went for our first meal. The dining hall housed the 60 students for all meals. I soon found out that mealtimes were not quite what I had expected. The dining room was large and sounds echoed. People talked loudly across the tables to each other. After spending so many years living on my own, and enjoying peaceful mealtimes, this seemed alien to me. Also it seemed as if there was always a crush to get the food and a rush to eat – no leisurely mealtimes here! That was my first culture shock. I soon found a way of overcoming it; in part, anyway. I decided that I would not go to the dining hall for all my meals. Each day I missed either the lunch or the evening meal and bought snacks to eat in my room instead. I found these times so valuable; I could stay in my room, and have some peace and quiet when everybody else was in the dining hall. I felt that I was desperately grabbing at precious moments.

I felt, too, that the attitude was authoritarian and the discipline hard, especially for me – a mature student. For years previously I had been given a lot of freedom in the work I had done, and had responsibility to work on my own initiative. As I am a self-motivated person, I did not like the strict hours and timetables now imposed upon me. It went against the grain to have a morning bell to wake me up; in fact, it was a shock to my system! I felt I was mature enough to be responsible for my own timekeeping, and anyway I was always awake before the bell. I found it humiliating to have to put up with this awful old school bell clang-clang, clanging along the corridors and outside my door!

Spending some time here would ease me gently back into life, I thought, but actually the experience was more akin to being thrown in at the deep end of life, after spending a year at home, resting and relaxing and with no commitment to any work situation. The pace was fast, with lots to accomplish in the allotted time, and the timetable was set so that almost all my time was accounted for, leaving little space to think and reflect. I found the strict discipline quite demotivating, as I do not work well under conditions where there is great pressure for quantities of work to be done – rather, I am most creative when given lots of space and responsibility. My year here in this most beautiful place was one of the toughest tests I have ever endured in my life, and I was determined to see it through – and that I did. I am not one to give up easily, I will not be defeated, and soon I settled in to lectures, worship and manual work.

One of the disciplines of the college is that everybody is given some manual work to do for two afternoons each week. I soon discovered that my task was to work with two other students in the chapel. It was a small chapel, with pews and some small stained glass windows running down each side. When we met for the first time together to discuss our manual duties, I felt very privileged to be able to spend time in the chapel, and to look after this special part of the college. We were each, in turn, to be on duty in the vestry or on the door, for each of the services, prayer times and other meetings, and we were to keep the chapel clean and tidy. It worked out well for me because it was more flexible than a lot of the other jobs that were given to students. The fact that we were on duty each morning in the vestry to pray for the people leading prayers, meant that on the cleaning days, once we had done our cleaning, we were free. Between the three of us, we divided the cleaning into our own small jobs and so twice each week I dusted the pews, tidied the hymn books and cleaned the windows. I was so grateful that this task was quite light and easy.

Although one would imagine that the timetable of events would provide a form of security, it had the opposite effect upon me. The fact that anything could be changed without a moment's notice and without consultation made me feel insecure. There was a sense of unpredictability and uncertainty, as if I had no control over the events, and that was hard.

There were lighter moments, though. Wednesday afternoons were free and I often drove into Bakewell with one or two friends. We would meander round the charity shops, looking for bargains, or sit by the river and watch the ducks and swans, or just enjoy a few hours of freedom. We called these afternoons 'The Bakewell Blitz' because we packed so much into them.

An added pressure during my year was that I had decided to apply again to become a minister. All through the process I felt sure that this was what God wanted me to do. I kept giving it over to God, and was prepared, this second time, to accept whatever decision was made. I made it through to the April Committee, the final interviewing stage. When I received the letter bringing the disappointing news that I would not be accepted, I wondered why I had had to go through that whole process again, only to be turned down at the last hurdle. One reason may have been that at all the interviews with panels of different people at each stage, I was asked to share my recent experience. In fact, this was a tremendous opportunity to witness to the power of God, to many people within the Church. That may have been the only reason that I went through it all, but I will never know. One thing I do know is that after my disappointment, I knew God was saying to me 'Go home from Cliff College and wait. Then I will tell you.' It was as if I needed to finish this course first, before I would know the next move. It was as if God was saying that I had no need to worry about what happens next, but to just concentrate on what I was doing now. So it seemed that I had to finish my course at college, and then go home, when the next move would be revealed.

Part of the course at Cliff College takes students on mission during the year, and with my Easter mission over, which was a ten-day mission, I now had the summer mission to prepare for, which was for three weeks in July. To my delight, I was chosen to be part of the Isle of Man team. My mother was of Manx origin, and so I decided to take the opportunity to find out more about my relatives on the island whilst there.

Packing our bags to depart on this final mission of the year gave an air of excitement to the team. It was a beautiful morning when we set off in three cars, luggage and equipment crammed between eight people bound for the ferry at Heysham. Once off the ferry at Douglas, after a smooth crossing, it did not take us long to travel to Ramsey where our base was to be. We were met by people from the church in one of the houses, and were given a meal. I was staying in a house situated directly on the promenade, facing out to sea, and so could smell the freshness of the salt air, and hear the waves lashing onto the beach. This was particularly beautiful at night, especially when it was clear and the moon was bright. Thankfully, I was able to locate some of my relatives. It happened on one of our days off when it was a special holiday for the Manx; Tynwald day, when the Manx Parliament meets on the top of Tynwald Hill. On this day there are celebrations all over the island. I was invited to a garden party by one of the church members, whom I had met from the south of the island. She knew my family and informed me that some of them would be there at the garden party. That was a very special day.

I wondered why I had been brought to this most beautiful island, and I was constantly aware that I needed to seek out the direction for the rest of my life. So when I found out that there was going to be a job advertised in the near future for a lay-worker on the island, I pricked up my ears. This post would be for someone to look after a group of churches, almost like the job of a minister. The person in the post at the time was leaving, so I decided to ask some questions, and discovered I was very interested in applying. I felt it would suit me well, and so spent some time with the superintendent minister, asking questions. The post was to be advertised later that year, and I decided to apply. Is this why I was brought to the island, I wondered. How wonderful to be able to live here! Life was at a pace much slower than on the mainland, it was easy, relaxed and felt good. There definitely was a sense of freedom on the island, no rush or pressure. In fact we learnt that Manx time meant that every event started at least five minutes late! Life was safe and secure; there was hardly any crime. Apart from in Douglas, people could safely leave the doors of their houses and cars unlocked. It was such a wonderful and peaceful place to live, almost like another world and the people were incredibly friendly and helpful. I pondered on this, and during the time I spent there, I dreamt of living there; to me it seemed like heaven, and I felt it would be just right for me. As I drove round the island, and became familiar with the locations of the churches and the people, I really believed that this was what I should do next. It seemed an achievable goal, something I was capable of and would enjoy. God's words echoed in my mind: that I should go home first, and then I would know. I had nearly finished the course, and this was the last lap. I took this idea of my future home with me and told no one; I just decided to wait and see. The Isle of Man mission was a very positive experience, as I had been given opportunities to take responsibility for many different events. I felt I had been trusted, and that is when I excel – when I am given lots of scope and freedom.

Prize-giving day at Cliff College was special. It was held on a Sunday, with friends and family invited. As we received our certificates, we felt good that we had achieved something (and I was delighted with my 2:1). Some students would be moving on into jobs, some would be going back to their old jobs, and some were still searching. Some would be coming back for another year. It was sad and happy at the same time, and tears were shed as we said our goodbyes to those we had spent our lives with for the past few months. As I ventured home again, God's words still kept echoing in my mind: that I should go home first, and then I would know His plan.

17

Birthday

The next important event in my life – a week after returning from Cliff College – was my birthday. I was going to be 50 years old and I had decided to make it special. A couple of years earlier, a friend of mine, Ian, who is a local preacher, had a service of thanksgiving for his 50 years of life. I thought it was a brilliant idea, and so asked him if he would lead a service for me. I felt that to have a celebration of thanksgiving for my life was so apt. Certainly, almost two years after my life had been saved in such a remarkable way, I wanted to give thanks in this overt way as a witness to the people who would attend.

I particularly wanted to thank my friends from my own church, and my family, for all their support over the past months and years, and especially for their prayers. The day soon dawned, and it was a moving service for me as I recalled how so many of these people had prayed for me, each in their own special way. We sang, prayed, listened to soloists, and to Ian speaking about the love of God and the meaning of life. Ian wrote a hymn which we sang at this service.

Lord of our lives, we come to you for guidance;
Guidance to live as you would have us live.
Show us your will, and make us ever willing
Your work to do, your Kingdom to proclaim.

Lord who is mighty, Lord who is good,
We praise and worship, the God whose name is Love.

Lord of our lives, we come to you for leading
O'er earth's green fields and oceans' sandy shore.
How strong the truth whose blessed strains are telling
Of that new life when sin shall be no more.
Lord who is mighty, Lord who is good,
We praise and worship, the Lord whose name is Love.

Lord of our lives, we come to you for loving,
Knowing your love is till our lives shall end.
May we be blessed as in our obligation.
We love our friends as you would have us love.
Lord who is mighty, Lord who is good,
We praise and worship, the Lord whose name is Love.

Lord of all power, the King of all creation,
Give us the strength to always do your will.
May we be never dull or fail to follow
With willing feet the pathway you have trod.
Lord who is mighty, Lord who is good,
We praise and worship, the Lord whose name is Love.[1]

Then we had a buffet meal where we all mingled and chatted, and introductions were made. Although strangers to each other, *all* were known to me in some way – all these individual people had played such an important part in my life.

Eventually, everyone departed, except for my cousin from Liverpool who came home with me. As we sat talking, I remembered that I had thought about Liverpool quite a lot over the past week, and I found myself feeling that God wanted me to be in Liverpool. Why, I did not know. But my cousin said that she had had the same idea. But what was I to do in Liverpool? Was this God speaking? What about the Isle of Man?

When my cousin left, I opened the myriads of cards I had received and counted the cash and cheques that I had asked to be donated to Victim Support and to the Church. Then I retired to bed. I started to settle down to sleep, but it was late and I found it difficult to be calm after all the activity of the day. Racing in my mind were thoughts of Liverpool and then thoughts of the Isle of Man. I slept fitfully. Then at 1 a.m. I was awoken by noise. There were men working on the railway and I could hear the sounds of drills whirring, and machinery clanking.

Through the night I wrestled, my mind whirring like the machines, my mind unsettled, searching and wondering. Thoughts of that wonderful time in the Isle of Man kept recurring, thoughts of Liverpool kept appearing. 'God, what do you want me in Liverpool for?' I demanded. 'I won't be safe in Liverpool.' I had known, for a long time, that whatever else I did in my life, I was to work with victims of crime. I had had so much help from Victim Support, and I had seen a need there not previously known by me, that I determined to help in some way. The most obvious way was to volunteer to help others who were victims of crime. 'But Liverpool?' I questioned. A picture emerged in my mind, of me standing in a street in Liverpool. 'Well, what next? I can't just go there and stand in the street,' I muttered out loud to God, feeling very insecure and nervous about going to this city where there is so much crime. But then I realized that if I am to work with victims of crime, there is no point in going somewhere like the Isle of Man where there is virtually no crime. What use would I be there? There is a need in Liverpool.

By now it was four o'clock in the morning and I still had not slept. Dawn was just breaking. I looked out of the window. I love the view from my bedroom window. In the daytime I can see the massive satellite dish at Jodrell Bank, looking on the skyline, reflecting the sun and beaming like another sun. I could not see Jodrell Bank now, because it was still too dark. What I could see was a bright morning star. In fact it was the planet Venus, but to me it looked like a star, big and bright, shining as a portent to me. There was also a new moon in the sky. The sky was bright and clear and I knew. I knew that God wanted me to go to Liverpool. Yet I needed to be sure. I decided I would still pursue the Isle of Man post, so that I would be sure of my direction, but somehow, I could tell that it was Liverpool where God wanted me to be planted.

I recalled that all through my year at Cliff College we had sung a song that echoed the words of Samuel, when God called him in the night. Now I was aware that many people would be crying out for help, for the loving arms of Jesus to be put around them, to hold them up in their time of need in the city of Liverpool. All I could say was 'Here I am, Lord.'

My friend Pauline had said to me that there would be a wide and effective door open for me. She was right. I went to Liverpool to make some enquiries about the need in the area, and found that there was a great need for people to work with victims. I found that Liverpool was a city leading the way in reconciliation, especially reconciliation between the churches, and it was a place which had made so much progress in the past few decades since I had been there as a child. What better place for me to be, where forgiveness and reconciliation was materializing in abundance? To work in the Isle of Man was tempting, it would have been an attractive, cosy, comfortable and easy option, but it would not have been enabling me to live life to the full. I may have felt relaxed and happy, but not challenged. Living life to the full means being obedient to God, and that often means living on the edge, taking risks and stepping out into the unknown. To go to Liverpool meant living by faith – there would be no paid job.

Walking the streets of Liverpool was frightening. I had to pray every step I took. It has made me realize that I need to rely on God every moment. I have talked to many people who have become victims of crime, and who have shared their needs. What I feel I can do most of all is to pray for them, whether they know this or not, whether I pray with them or silently in my heart.

City churches are so very different from those in rural settings and I have been heartened by the openness to experimenting with different styles of worship. I believe I was sent to Liverpool 'for a season', just for a short period of time so that I could know in my heart the needs of the city. I believe that there were specific reasons for me to go there. I was a link in a chain, a connection which enabled certain things to happen.

Now, after spending almost a year in Liverpool, I feel God is moving me on to something new and so at the time of writing I am taking some time out to reflect upon what God wants for me next. I feel sure that there are many more insights to develop from the experience I had, which are deep within me, so I am continuing to express these in writing. I am also training to be a counsellor. I must, however, get my priorities right and the most important thing for me to do is to love God. Whatever else I do is secondary.

Notes

1. Hymn written by Ian D. Lee, 1994.

18

Signs and Wonders

Many amazing and mysterious events have occurred since my encounter with God on the day I was attacked, and I have no explanation for them. But I know that they are important, even if for one reason only, and that is to witness to the world about the power of God.

Many people prayed for me, especially in those first few days, and one lady whom I did not know was walking near to the place where I was attacked, just three days later. Whilst she was walking she was praying for me, looking at the direction where my attack took place. Sadly, she then became another victim of rape and during her incident, she also had a vision, one of Jesus on the cross with her alongside Him. To me that communicated her suffering alongside me. The ultimate in prayer is to be immersed in the situation with the person and that is what happened to her. As Jesus was alongside her, she was alongside me in my suffering. Such depth of prayer is very powerful.

Sharing my experience with others has been, and is continuing to be, a most powerful tool, pouring out the power of God to others and providing healing. I do not know why or how this happens but it does. This has occurred so many times now, and yet each time I am still amazed at the effect it has on people.

One such incident happened when I was in Llandudno at a conference, run for a women's group. I expected it to be a good time of fellowship and fun, which needless to say it was, but it turned out to be much more than that. The conference leaders were a minister and his wife and the subject was the suffering or passion of Christ, and ours. I sat in awe and wonder, realizing that every word was important and relevant to my experience. It was as if the programme had been specially written for me. They talked about how we share in Christ's life and in all aspects of the gospel, especially in the suffering. This truth had been revealed to me already, as I have explained. I shared with the minister what had happened to me, and how I had realized that I had personally experienced the cross with Jesus; he was greatly moved. In fact it was he who brought me to realize that the word 'passion' means 'to be handed over'. We prayed together. In the next session of the conference we were asked to go into groups, and to tell each other of any profound experiences which have helped us to learn about ourselves through suffering. I just had to share with my group what had happened to me. When we joined together again to summarize our time together, we were asked if we could express what we discussed. My heart was pounding and I knew I had to speak out. I stood up and told the whole group what had happened to me, and that through this horrific experience I had shared the suffering and the cross with Christ. I also asked people to pray for my attacker. Later that day I found out that it had had a profound effect on many people. It was as if the Holy Spirit moved across the room and into the hearts of people, like a rushing wind, and all I did was to tell them what happened.

Later I sat at lunch with three women from London, who had remembered the incident on the news but did not know me, one of whom said that she had been praying for me. That lunch was amazing. I did not mean to share so much, but it all came pouring out, and everyone was either in tears or on the verge of tears. The Holy Spirit was touching us all. God surely brought us together. I felt so aware of the awesome power that was flowing through me, it was rather frightening. One or two people commented on the fact that it was wonderful the way I could forgive my attacker, and yet I had not specifically said that I had forgiven him. When I asked how they knew, they said it was obvious, it just showed. I awoke at 2 a.m. the following morning and just sat staring, wide awake, in amazement at the power of the Holy Spirit. In the darkness, I saw an illuminating light pouring out.

Then began a series of events which led to my story being shared with many thousands of people. In recent years I have taken part in a mission programme called 'Share Jesus' organized by the Rev Dr Rob Frost. This is a week-long mission, held in various parts of the country, which involves meeting with a group and spending a week living in the church, camping on the premises, and taking part in the life of the Church in whatever way they need. A number of groups are placed in different churches in one area. I was placed at Daventry on this particular mission, and on the first Sunday was asked to preach in the evening. I decided to preach about forgiveness, and to share my story within the sermon. The next day one of the co-ordinators came to visit the church, and to ask if there were any particularly powerful stories which could be used at the big celebration on the Wednesday evening. Someone told him my story, he made a note and inevitably I was asked to share at the big celebration where I was interviewed by Rob Frost.

This led to Rob asking me to take part in a radio interview on his programme on a Sunday evening in November, which I did. In turn, this led to him asking me to speak at 'Easter People', a massive conference which was being held that year at Blackpool. At the Saturday night main event he interviewed me again, and then spoke about how God can use people if they are willing to be used. As the conference was in Blackpool in the midst of the fairground, Rob talked about the roller coaster. He explained that just as when riding on a roller coaster, we need in life to have something to hang on to; similarly, living in a roller-coaster world we need to have fixed points to focus on. He suggested that these fixed points were essential, and that it is important to focus on a vision of Jesus, a vision of need in the world, a vision of ourselves, not as we see ourselves, but as *God* sees us, and a vision of the Holy City.

Every time I sit and share my story with someone, something profound happens. One day when I had an interview at the job centre, I had not intended to share my story because I didn't think it would be necessary, but the clerk asked why I had been claiming sickness benefit for such a long period of time. So I told her. She sat with her mouth open and could not believe that she was looking at a miracle. Another time when I was in the Isle of Man on a mission, I was enjoying a hot drink after a swim when a man came to sit at the table with me. I picked up a newspaper and on the front page was the terrible news of a child's murder. We started talking about this, and it led to me telling my story once again. He sat there astounded, his mouth gaping open wide. He said, 'Well, I've read about people like you but have never met one.' I'm not sure what he meant by 'one'. He was looking at a miracle and it showed. I walked away with a smile on my face, and a great sense of the power and the peace of God within me.

Friday is now a special day for me. I remember when I had been at Cliff College for a week; it was a Friday morning and when I awoke I knew full well that this particular Friday was going to be emotionally demanding. It was one year since my attack. One year to the day, not the date. I felt uneasy because, as far as I knew, most of the people at college did not know much about me. I wondered how I was going to cope that day, and decided to try to dismiss it, put it to one side and perhaps deal with it later. Over the months since the attack, especially to begin with, Fridays were a constant reminder of the incident, but over time the vivid memories diminished.

However, this Friday was significant. I felt scared. Nothing could have prepared me for what was about to happen. I walked into morning prayers in the chapel and staring me in the face was something quite astonishing. The acetate projected on to the screen was powerful. It was a collage of newspaper cuttings and headlines and the words which stood out were 'murder', 'rape' and 'hell'. Yet there were other words too which were positive. The word 'beautiful' was written across the middle and the word 'heaven' was clearly noticeable. I was speechless because the words in front of me were so relevant to me. Newspaper headlines had been difficult for me to read over many months. Whilst I was in hospital I was protected from all the news in the press and on television, and indeed there was quite a lot of publicity about my case, also considering the fact that another woman was raped just three days after me. Programmes about rape and about forgiveness were screened because of these incidents. I did not see any of the newspapers for a good many weeks, and eventually when the police sent me all the press cuttings, I sat and read them and was quite horrified at what was written. It was strange reading about myself in the newspaper, and especially reading about such an horrific incident. It was as if I was facing up to the seriousness of the situation at a deeper level. After that I found it difficult to read newspapers for a long time.

Now, right in front of my eyes, was a collage of newspaper headlines clearly depicting the words 'heaven' and 'hell'. The image showed good and bad. I could not believe what I saw, because it spoke in words what I had experienced on that day of my attack: my awareness of heaven and hell simultaneously; my awareness of such violence and confusion and yet peace and enlightenment. Then the student, who was leading prayers, spoke from the Bible those words from Genesis: 'While a wind from God swept over the face of the waters' (1:2). These were the very words I had been using in my story over the year to explain how God was with me, hovering over the mess and hell that I was experiencing during the rape. And all this was presented on this significant day for me. I was speechless and said nothing to anyone. However, later that day after evening prayers I sat with two lovely ladies and started to cry, because the emotion was just overwhelming. I told my story and they were amazed. I found out later that the student who had led prayers that morning had agonized over what to say and do for days. God was speaking to him, and he allowed God to use him for me that day.

God clearly spoke to me through this, because at the beginning of the day I had decided to try to dismiss the whole incident. But God had other plans. I knew that I was not to forget it, but to remember it, to celebrate it, and this was a sign. Just as when the Jews were to remember that day when God brought them out of Egypt, that day of liberation, with Moses leading them, and celebrate the Passover, I am to remember the day that God saved me and brought me new life.

Now I know that on 23 September every year I have to remember particularly that day, and to celebrate it in some way. I am intending to spend the day in prayer especially to pray for my attacker, but also to pray for all victims. My prayer is that people will be able to forgive each other. I know that God is powerful, and that He is using the events of my life in a profound way, without my even trying.

19

Endings and Beginnings

To Weavers Everywhere

God sits weaving.
The beautiful creation tapestry She wove with such joy is mutilated, torn into shreds,
Reduced to rags,
Its beauty fragmented by force.
God sits weeping.
But, look, She is gathering up the shreds to weave something new.
She gathers our shreds of sorrow, the pain, the tears, the frustration caused by cruelty.
Crushing, ignoring, violating, killing.
She gathers the rags of hard work, attempts at advocacy, initiatives for peace, protests against injustice.
All the seemingly little and weak words and deeds offered sacrificially in hope, in faith, in love.
And look, She is weaving them all with golden threads of jubilation into a new tapestry, a creation richer, more beautiful than the old one was.

God sits weaving, patiently, persistently, with a smile that radiates like a rainbow on her tear streaked face.

> And She invites us, not only to keep offering her the shreds and rags of our suffering and our work, but even more, to take our place beside her at the jubilee loom,
> And weave with her the tapestry of the new creation.[1]

Life has to move on. I am a realist: my life was shattered, but has been woven back together in a remarkable way. I have been scarred both physically – I have the scar where the dagger went in and the ten-inch scar from my life-saving operation – and mentally. Those scars will remain with me for the rest of my life, and I will remember the events that caused the scars clearly, However, the mental scars have not, and I trust never will, fester. They are healed, but remain as a constant reminder that one specific Friday in my life, God intervened in a most remarkable way. Like someone tearing apart a precious and delicate rosebud, my life was wrecked with savagery. Once the bud is destroyed, there can be no flower, but *I* was not destroyed. God recreated the shattered and broken petals of my life, and now a fragrance is emitted.

If I look at myself through the eyes of the world and its pressures, maybe some people would perceive that I am not healed. But I am healed in a way far beyond the understanding of most people. The establishment is guilty of setting standards unnatural for humanity, and I refuse to be pressured into living my life the way the world wants me to live, in the fast lane. As far as God is concerned, I am healed, healed to do His work in the way that He wants; healed to be the person He wants me to be as a new creation. The scars remain to remind me that on that Friday I met with the Lord Jesus Christ, and experienced insights into His love that were incredible, and I am privileged to have had that experience. The immense, immeasurable love God showed me is for every single person on earth, no matter how vile or evil they may be. The love of God poured out, not just on the man who attacked me, but to the whole of humanity, and is still pouring out. I saw that God would never let him go, no matter what he had done in the past, was doing in the present, or would do in the future. I saw that God loves every human being in such a profound and amazing way that He will never let any human being go. He will always enfold all people in the arms of love and compassion for ever. What a revelation!

It has been a long, hard road, and I believe in some areas of my life it will continue to be arduous, as I will always have the memories of such an horrific incident in my life. Healing takes time, and it was three months after the *Crime Monthly* programme that I had the courage to sit down and watch the video. I arranged to watch it with Christina, feeling secure with her, knowing that she would be able to handle with me any of the emotions I might have to deal with. It was important for me to be able to watch the video, so that I could put that behind me. My hesitancy to watch the film emerged from the day when I took part in the filming, when I had been greatly disturbed, seeing the face of the actor playing the part of my attacker. I felt nervous because I did not know how I would react. In a way I was frightened of the fear I might feel, but I could not ignore the fact that the video was there, and I wanted to watch it so that if any emotions had not been dealt with, then perhaps they would emerge at this stage, and I could then deal with them. Christina also felt nervous, and I realized that it takes a lot of courage to enter into the darkness of something so horrific. I had also delayed watching the video for one other more objective reason, and that was that I was concerned that my mind might be contaminated with the images from the video reconstruction and that the real drama might fade. This may have caused a problem if and when I needed to appear in court. However, I came to the decision that I must put my healing first. The video was quite specific with a reconstruction of the rape in detail, as they needed to show the man with no clothes on to reveal identifying tattoos on his body. As the video ran and showed the man's face in close up, I jumped in terror; the likeness was uncanny. I coped, though, and was satisfied that I was able to watch a re-run of the scene, knowing that it was an important part of my healing. Another hurdle was over.

Learning to live with the fact that my attacker may never be found is hard, and it took a long time to come to terms with this fact. I felt frustrated for so long, because I wanted him to be caught so that he could get help, but then I realized that God could work in his life through other routes, and he could be getting help or love from someone already. I did not want the man found because I wanted revenge, I wanted him caught so that he could be helped. Finally, I had to let that go, although the search is continuing, and all I could do was to pray for him and continue to pray that he will not harm anyone else.

Pressures from well-meaning friends were very real, and it seemed as if some people were waiting for me to have some sort of breakdown, but I did not. Right from the beginning people expected me to show anger, and were convinced that I was suppressing this emotion. People warned me to be careful in case I experienced a delayed reaction, because I was coping so well. I began to believe this myself, but the negative emotions were just not there. My job was to love and to realize healing. God had given me the gifts of love, forgiveness and life.

The pressure of so much contact with the police was a burden. There was no way I could even think of putting the whole affair behind me. As I write this book my attacker has not been found and so the file is still open, but during the time that the investigation was 'fully fledged' I needed to let the police know exactly where I was at any time, so that I could be contacted immediately in the event of my being needed to identify anyone who was arrested. Even when I went on holiday abroad, I knew that they might want to contact me and might need to fly me back home. This was a constant burden and, of course, a constant reminder of the incident.

Frustration grabbed me time after time as people, in everyday conversations, talked about trivia. All I wanted to discuss was deep, profound and meaningful truths and realities. I began to feel isolated, as, in my own world, I shut myself off from what seemed to me to be of little consequence. This frustration is often still with me.

Demands from other people were, not surprisingly, very difficult to cope with. In the early days everyone wanted to see me, and I found it very hard to cope with that. What I really wanted was to take myself to some remote place, and be completely on my own, but this was not possible. For one reason I did not feel confident enough, and another was that at that time the police needed to have contact and easy access to me. I began to feel trapped, and the stress was apparent. Although I desired to be alone, my friends were very important to me, and I needed to be able to talk to people, so there was conflict in my mind and that was not easy. Only time dispersed these feelings, although I still do need to spend quite lengthy periods of time on my own.

As time moved on I was able to face reading the newspapers again and to listen when people told me of other serious crimes. My healing became apparent as I was able to cope with the stories people told, especially ones which were close to home. In a strange way I was jealous of media coverage when anything major happened, and I think it was because I was still seeing my own experience as so vitally important to me. Inside I was silently screaming.

Fear was the biggest emotion I had to deal with, and it was two years after the event that God showed me it was the right time to bring it to the surface. In a prayer time with friends we asked God to reveal the root of my fear. I found that it had been passed on from my mother when I was a baby, and I had lived with fear of so many things for 50 years. Now I was able to hand it over to God. Later I realized that fear is a part of life that will not go away. 'Courage is simply the willingness to be afraid and act anyway.'[2] I learned that my fear would never dissolve, but that I would need to have the courage and take action in spite of the fear, if I was going to live a full life. God revealed also that I had allowed myself to be a victim all my life, and that this was related to the fear because I had been afraid to speak out and so, consequently, fell into the role of victim, always putting up with what others wanted, and not speaking out for myself. I had now been through an experience whereby I was labelled a 'victim', and that helped me to realize more fully how I had allowed myself to fall into the victim role in many other areas of my life. All the people involved at the scene of the crime were victims in one sense. I have heard it said that a witness to violence is a victim of violence.

Three victims we became that day
The evil man – how could he love
He did not know
Goodness – a victim of circumstance
Watching in horror and helpless too
And I,
the victim in the eyes of the world.

I had come a long way along the road to healing in that area in recent years, but the attack on my life had set me back, and my confidence had been shattered. Like the tearing of my clothes, the bud had been torn apart, but God recreated a new flower.

Many people live their lives as a victim of what society, their family or their partner expects of them. This can never be right, because God has made each one of us unique and to find our true selves is very important. Anything less than that means we are not valuing ourselves. How can we offer ourselves to God, if we do not know who we are or our value? It is God's desire that we become self-aware, and love ourselves as He loves us. The teaching of the Church is often misunderstood, and leads people to believe that they are worthless and of little or no value, considering that to be what God wants. But Jesus said that we are to love our neighbours as ourselves, and so we must learn truly to love ourselves.

The way to freedom from fear of the future lies in the presence of this living, transforming Christ, who has the power to unlock our doors, to stand with us, to assure us of His peace and to touch our lives. His living presence assures us that nothing that can happen in the future can separate us from Him.

To go out into the world and tell of what God has done for me has not been easy. Every time I tell my story, I have to re-live it and it costs, but that is what God wants – what else can I do? I have often desired to take myself away and hide from the world, just living a quiet life, alone. Yet God keeps calling me out from my cocoon, calling me out into the rain. I believe it is of the utmost importance to spend time alone with God, and I am realizing more and more that for me it is an essential part of the Christian life. To spend quality time with God is not the same as hiding from life or refusing to face life. I was caught in a heavy shower of rain one day, just walking from the car to a house. Standing by the door waiting for the door to open, I became soaked as I had no coat and no umbrella. This is what God does: He calls us outside, for that is where He wants us to be, not hiding in some safe place, but out in the world, as a presence within the world, amongst the people who are crying out in desperation.

The story of Lazarus being raised from the dead (John 11:38–44), revealed much to me when I was meditating on this event. When John talks of signs and wonders, the miracles that Jesus performed, he means that they are windows which enable us to see the glory of God. The miracles demonstrate the glory of Christ breaking into time and into human affairs. These windows enable us to see into eternity. The story of Lazarus is not just about the physical coming back to life of one person, it is about Jesus offering life in all its fullness to each one of us. I invite you to immerse yourselves into the story and picture the scene of Lazarus in the tomb, which is so dark and black that you cannot even see your hands in front of your face. There is a cave, with a stone blocking out the light. It is cold, eerie and the darkness is thick and silent. This is a place which represents where many of us actually like to stay in life, because even though it is unpleasant, the familiarity is comforting. To be left alone and away from the noise and demands of the world in this tomb is a safe haven, it's the easy option. But in staying in that tomb, we become dead in our own selfishness, in our own unforgiveness and in our own guilt. We experience a mentally torturous hell and death.

Then in the midst of the blackness suddenly a light breaks into the tomb. Jesus breaks into our lives. The stone has been rolled away, and now we see light which we cannot ignore, as it is filling the tomb with an illuminating radiance. Then we hear the voice of Jesus shouting loudly, 'Lazarus, come out.' (You could imagine Jesus calling your own name here.) We slowly get ourselves up, and move one step at a time towards the doorway and the light, which is so bright it frightens us. As we move out into the powerful, beaming light, the grave clothes begin to loosen and we hear the voice of Jesus saying, 'Take off the grave clothes.' The nearer we get to Jesus, the brighter the light becomes, and the clothes fall off as we move, to reveal what we are. We become aware of things which need to be put right, in the presence of Jesus, because He knows all things, and can see through our pain. He can see through our bitterness; He can see through our despair; He can see our true selves. As we come into the presence of Jesus, feel those grave clothes falling off and experience the freedom that it brings, then picture falling at His feet in repentance, realizing your weaknesses and failings. Because His power is so great and His presence so awesome, we receive healing. We cannot help it, the unforgiveness melts away, the unloving nature melts away and the bitterness melts away. We are being healed.

I was in that tomb, metaphorically, at the time I faced death, yet the light shone upon me and Jesus called me back to life. It was frightening and awesome to see the power that drew me out, but I could not ignore the call. Amazingly, as we are healed ourselves, we find that without knowing it we are vessels for the work of Christ, by being something God has made us, and by being Jesus to others. That is my ultimate aim, to *be* the person God wants me to *be*.

As I regained my confidence I began to take more risks and I found that I forgot to be afraid in circumstances which previously I had approached with trepidation. The fear of doing new things will never go away, but confidence is gained by having the courage to go ahead, to move out into the unknown, in spite of the fear. I am a person with a strong sense of pictures as analogies. I imagined myself to be a galleon sailing on the sea and moving out further and further into uncharted waters. I then put up more sails, so that the wind would take me out further to more adventures. As I put up the sails and moved out and risked more, then I began to move out and slowly those things that once seemed risky, did not feel risky any more. The wind that blows me along is the power of the Holy Spirit. But I am the galleon and I am also at the wheel, controlling the rudder, so whatever comes my way, it is up to me to steer it. I believe this is what I do. I believe that through my life I have always turned negative situations and experiences to good use, and used those circumstances as stepping stones. Life is to be lived to the full, to be enjoyed and to be loved.

When the galleon is in calm waters, with a gentle breeze, easy to steer or guide, we relax and take things easy. But we are not moving very much. When the wind or the power comes in force, then the galleon moves on and forward with speed, but with it comes big waves and we need energy, wisdom and to be alert, otherwise a wave could capsize the vessel. We have a choice – to put up our sails and go with the wind, or to leave our sails down and go nowhere. We have a choice, to follow God, or to go our own way.

Notes

1. Reinstrar, M., Quoted in *Faith and Worship*, Peterborough, Methodist Publishing House, Unit 6.
2. Hamachek, Don, *Encounters with the Self*, USA, Rinehart and Winston, Inc., 1992, p. 336.

Epilogue

A symphonic resonance of orchestral delights with ordered string and wind instruments conducted precisely in tune. Is that an accurate description of God? Or is your analogy more like that of a jazz band, with no apparent order, each instrument seemingly playing their own tune with an individuality and uniqueness expressed by each player? Certainly the God of the universe, the author of the heavens and the earth created order out of chaos, but an order that allows freedom and expression. God is the God of the universe, He is unpredictable and cannot be constrained to any box-like image. There are no easy answers as to why things happen in a certain way. Only God knows. The point is that when we have faith in Him, whatever happens in our lives can be coped with; He will see us through the most difficult and horrendous times.

People may ask why I lived when others died. I believe that I lived so that I would be able to tell of the mighty and wonderful acts of God, to tell of His glory and the miracle in my life. I believe, though, that ultimate healing is death from this life, and the transition into the next life, where we will have no pain or suffering, no anguish or fear. That is heaven.

Since that day no tree has ever looked the same to me. No copse or woodland can ever be the same. As I look at stretches of woodland, I see them as potential plots for the experiences of life. I see the horrific things of life, but also I see the potential beauty and magnificence, and the vision in it all. Each leaf on every tree is like a poem, pronouncing in a way that words cannot, some profound truth about life.

Every leaf is a poem,
hanging on the tree.
Every blossom a song
ringing sweet melody.

Each tree is an orchestra,
a living vibrant theme,
as the wind blows through branches
conducting the tune.

Music of the rustling
words of whistling
ring into my ears
and I hear the giant sing.

Crying sombre bass notes
with sad faces of the world
screaming loud high pitches
for the people so oppressed.

Yet dancing and rejoicing
that so many are set free.
Come and join the orchestra
Of life and liberty.

As I write these words I am reflecting on almost three years of my journey of healing, and the world is looking forward to the millennium. Many people are making a stand to encourage countries to cancel the debts of other countries at the turn of the century, and I believe that would be a most significant and powerful force, enabling third world countries to have a chance to start again. My prayer is that people will forgive each other – individuals and countries – leaving behind the bitterness and hatred of the past, as we move on into the twenty-first century, to start a new life of peace together. My heart is sad when I read of people who cannot forgive, and who carry bitterness for many years in their hearts. I hope this book will help people who feel that they cannot forgive. I will pray for those people.

My plea is that you pray for my attacker – I do not know his name, and I do not know where he is, but I believe God touched him that day. I ask that you pray not just for that one man, but also for all the people represented by that man, who have become victims of a sick society. God shone light on that man, and I believe God is shining a most wondrous light on to the whole of the nation. That one man represented to me all the evil in the world.

The following prayer, written within the horrors of Ravensbruck Concentration Camp, is my prayer, and I hope will become your prayer too, especially if you are a victim of crime, a victim of oppression, or a victim of any other kind:

> O Lord, remember not only the men and women of good will, but also those of ill will. But do not remember all the suffering they have inflicted on us; remember the fruits we have bought, thanks to this suffering – our comradeship, our loyalty, our humility, our courage, our generosity, the greatness of heart which has grown out of all this; and when they come to judgement let all the fruits which we have borne be their forgiveness.[1]

If all this happened to me so that I would be able to share my story, to share my vision of God, then it was worth it. If all this happened to me so that one person is brought to know the love of Christ, then it was worth the pain and suffering endured.

Notes

1. Anonymous prayer from the concentration camp at Ravensbruck, c.1944. Quoted in *Just As I Am,* Ruth Etchells, London, Triangle Books, 1994, p. 92.